VARIABLE PASSIONS
A READING OF SHAKESPEARE'S
VENUS AND ADONIS

Variable Passions

A Reading of Shakespeare's *Venus and Adonis*

❖❖❖

❖

Anthony Mortimer

❖

AMS Press, Inc.

Library of Congress Cataloging-in-Publication Data

Mortimer, Anthony Robert.
  Variable passions: A reading of Shakespeare's Venus and Adonis / Anthony Mortimer.
    (AMS Studies in the Renaissance; no. 36)
    Includes bibliographical references and index.
    ISBN 0-404-62336-0 (hc.)
    1. Shakespeare, William, 1564-1616. Venus and Adonis. 2. English poetry—Italian influences. 3. Mythology, Classical, in literature. 4. Adonis (Greek deity) in literature. 5. Venus (Roman deity) in literature. I. Title. II. Series.
PR2845.M67   2000
821' .3—dc21   99-30572
                                                                CIP

All AMS Books are printed on acid-free paper that meets the guidelines for performance and durability of the Committee on Production Guidelines for Book Longevity of the Council on Library Resources.

Copyright © 2000 by AMS Press, Inc.
All rights reserved

AMS Press, Inc.
56 East 13th Street
New York, NY 10003-4686
U.S.A.

MANUFACTURED IN THE UNITED STATES OF AMERICA

for

MAYA

iuncta salus nostra est

Contents

Preface and Acknowledgments	ix
References and Abbreviations	xv
Chapter One Rhetoric, Myth and the Descent of Venus	1
Chapter Two "The Heart's Attorney": Venus as Wooer	37
Chapter Three "Danger Deviseth Shifts": Postponing the Boar	109
Chapter Four "With Him Is Beauty Slain": Death and Metamorphosis	131
Chapter Five Shakespeare and the Italian Tradition of Venus and Adonis	171
Bibliography	197
Index	209
Illustrations	107

Preface and Acknowledgments

I was probably somewhat older than the Gullio of the *Parnassus* plays, but still an undergraduate, when I read *Venus and Adonis* for the first time. Though I may not have kept the poem under my pillow, I do remember finding it a good deal more entertaining than critics and scholars had led me to believe it would or should be. This was a period (the late fifties) when the qualities most admired in poetry were suggested by adjectives like "crisp," "condensed," "tough" or even (God save the mark!) "masculine;" there seemed no way in which Shakespeare's narrative poems could be made to fit the bill and I decided not to advertise a pleasure that would have been as sure a sign of decadence as Aschenbach's indulgence in overripe strawberries.

The tide began to turn in the mid-seventies with stimulating essays by Lucy Gent, Richard Lanham and Coppelia Kahn, and with William Keach's groundbreaking *Elizabethan Erotic Narratives* (1977). The more recent work of Heather Dubrow, Jonathan Bate, Katherine Duncan-Jones and Catherine Belsey would suggest that the reputation of *Venus and Adonis* is still on the rise and that we now have a critical climate where a monograph study of the poem need not appear as a particularly eccentric enterprise. It is not hard to account for this increased interest in what had been for so long one of Shakespeare's most neglected works. One decisive factor is the considerable revival of interest in formal rhetoric, now seen as central to the whole intellectual achievement of the Renaissance rather than as an unfortunate habit which the modern reader must learn to tolerate. Another element in the poem's new status is the rise of what used to be feminist criticism and has now become "gender studies." Applied to Renaissance literature, such an approach has produced some very questionable results, but there can be little doubt that it has helped to move poems like *Venus and Adonis* from the margin to the center. Finally, uniting the two concerns, there is the recognition that, in sixteenth-century poetry, it is the specifically Ovidian genres of the erotic narrative and the female complaint that demonstrate the most complex and exemplary relations between rhetoric and gender.

My own reading of *Venus and Adonis* does, I hope, build on this foundation. My major concern, however, has been with the poem's mobility, with the extraordinarily flexible rhetoric that can apparently swing our responses from one extreme to the other within a single stanza or even a single line. This explains why I have taken the somewhat unfashionable option of devoting my three central chapters to what is, in effect, a running commentary. C. S. Lewis spoke of growing perplexity "as we read on;" but I believe that "reading on," if we do it carefully and slowly enough, will show us how the poem manages to contain its disturbing juxtapositions, its abrupt transitions, its rapid shifts in tone and perspective. In a recent book Eugene R. Kintgen has argued for the "radically analytical nature" of Tudor reading. Trained to derive pleasure from language deployed with self-conscious skill, readers would not go straight through a text, but rather take it in small concentrated doses, segment by segment, paying "close attention to language and style" and to "the speaker, the addressee, the time and the circumstances."[1] That is the kind of detailed rhetorical reading that *Venus and Adonis* demands and that I have attempted to provide—at the risk, no doubt, of sounding like E. K. glossing *The Shepheardes Calender* ("a prety Epanorthosis in these two verses, and withall a Paronomasia").[2] We may speak of "Shakespeare's narrative poems," but few readers would be attracted to *Venus and Adonis* by its

---

[1] Eugene R. Kintgen, *Reading in Tudor England* (Pittsburgh, 1996), 182–83.

[2] *Spenser's Minor Poems*, ed. Ernest de Sélincourt (Oxford, 1910), 17.

narrative sweep. Only when we look beyond mere narrative logic do we see that the poem has the same secretive ways of creating continuity that John Kerrigan finds in the *Sonnets*: "a rhythm, a rhyme, a quirk of syntax or an echoing image: such minutiae, hardly discernible in conscious reading, knit the poems together."[3] Part of my purpose is to make the minutiae discernible, and a book like Helen Vendler's *The Art of Shakespeare's Sonnets* (1997) has reassured me that this is no modest ambition. For all the large theoretical claims announced by so much contemporary work on Shakespeare, close sequential reading still has a great deal to offer.

In a broader context I have tried to show how the poem's mobility defeats allegory and how it embodies Shakespeare's delicately-balanced approach to the functions and relevance of myth. My final chapter contextualizes the poem in a new way and brings Shakespeare's achievement into sharper focus by seeing it in the light of half-a-dozen Italian versions of the same tale. We cannot hope to understand what Shakespeare does with the Ovidian erotic narrative unless we appreciate that he was working in an immensely popular European genre.

* * *

To write on any aspect of Shakespeare is to incur more debts than one can ever hope to acknowledge. This book probably has more than its fair share of insights originally borrowed from others and now so thoroughly absorbed that I feel them as my own. In my defense I can only plead that my bibliography makes up for a mountain of footnotes since it contains almost everything I have read on *Venus and Adonis* and certainly everything that I am conscious of having used. There are, of course, some books that have been more or less constantly at my elbow. The great *Variorum Edition* of Hyder Edward Rollins (1938) is a mine of information on the contemporary reception and critical history of *Venus and Adonis*. T. W. Baldwin's *On the Literary*

---

[3] Introduction to *Shakespeare's Sonnet and A Lover's Complaint*, New Penguin Shakespeare (Harmondsworth, 1986), 8.

Genetics of Shakspere's Poems and Sonnets (1950), despite what I regard as an overemphasis on Neoplatonism, remains an indispensable guide to the poem's literary background. I was lucky that John Roe's admirable New Cambridge edition (1992) appeared in time to save me from a number of errors that I would otherwise have made.

I am grateful to the University of Fribourg for allowing me nine months free from teaching and administration and to the University Council for a grant towards publication. It is also a pleasure to acknowledge the hospitality of the Warden and Fellows of Merton College, Oxford, where, as a Visiting Research Fellow, I enjoyed ideal conditions for work on this book. For permission to use revised versions of previously published material I must thank the editors of *English Studies* and *Colloquium Helveticum*.

I have accumulated considerable debts towards a number of friends and colleagues. John Carey was prodigal with kindnesses that he will soon forget and that I shall long remember; Robert Rehder was quietly and persistently supportive; David Colclough, on his way from Oxford to Cambridge, stopped off in Fribourg just long enough to become my first reader. Alessandro Martini and Simone de Reyff helped me to track down relevant Italian and French texts while Regina Schneider ensured a regular supply of photocopies from the Bodleian Library. My manuscript would never have reached anything like presentable form without the constant attention of Cristina Caiocca and the scrupulous professionalism of Ascension Nieto. The hospitality of Holger Klein enabled me to try out some of my ideas on his students in Salzburg. Katherine Duncan-Jones provided timely encouragement by sharing with me her own enthusiasm for the poem and by inviting me to participate in her seminar on the non-dramatic poems at the 26th Annual Meeting of the Shakespeare Association of America.

What I owe to Brian Vickers can only be measured by the condition of the manuscript that he returned to me after risking his digestion by reading it over the Christmas break. Hardly a page remained without his comment—generous in approval, frank in criticism and brimming with more good advice than I have had the wit to take. To find oneself in agreement with Brian Vickers is to gain a sudden access of confidence; to disagree with him is never less than a salutary experience.

Finally, there is the person to whom this book is dedicated. If, in this case, I do not acknowledge a debt, it is only because I have long since ceased to distinguish between what is mine and what is hers.

A. M.
Fribourg and Geneva, 1998

References and Abbreviations

For all poems and plays by Shakespeare I have used the *Oxford Shakespeare* (1986) edited by Stanley Wells and Gary Taylor. Line reference after citation is always to this edition. Where they were needed to indicate direct speech I have preserved quotation marks round indented citations. The text of *Venus and Adonis* presents very few problems and I have rarely needed to refer to Quarto spelling or punctuation. For Ovid and Virgil I give line reference to the Loeb editions which I have also used for the English translations. I have used the following abbreviations for important editions of *Venus and Adonis*:

Evans	Evans, Maurice, *The Narrative Poems*, New Penguin Shakespeare (Harmondsworth, 1989).
Roe	Roe, John, *The Poems*, New Cambridge Shakespeare (Cambridge, 1992).
Rollins	Rollins, Hyder Edward, *The Poems: A New Variorum Edition of Shakespeare* (Philadelphia, 1938).
Prince	Prince, F. T., *The Poems*, Arden Shakespeare (London, 1960).
Wells and Taylor	Wells, Stanley, and Gary Taylor, *The Oxford Shakespeare* (London, 1986).

Abbreviation of classical, Renaissance and Shakespearean titles follows standard practice.

1

Rhetoric, Myth and the Descent of Venus

It is difficult nowadays to imagine anyone making their first acquaintance with Shakespeare through the narrative poems. In 1593, however, although Shakespeare had already achieved a certain notoriety in the theater, the publication of *Venus and Adonis* gave an Elizabethan public their first opportunity to actually read his work. For the young dramatist the change of genre and the move from stage to page involved an appeal to the judgment of a more literate and sophisticated audience who, after Greene's virulent pamphlet, would be curious to see whether, in the cooler medium of print, there was more to the "upstart Crow" than resounding theatrical bombast.[1] The epigraph (from Ovid, *Amores*, I. xv. 35–36) is perfectly appropriate to the situation: *Vilia miretur vulgus: mihi flavus Apollo / Pocula Castalia plena ministret acqua* ("Let what is cheap excite the marvel

---

[1] "There is an upstart Crow, beautified with our feathers, that with his *Tygers hart wrapt in a Players hyde*, supposes he is as well able to bombaste out a blank verse as the best of you." Robert Greene, *Groats-worth of witte, bought with a million of Repentance* (London, 1592), sig. A3v. See Muriel C. Bradbrook, "Beasts and Gods: Greene's *Groats-Worth of Witte* and the Social Purpose of *Venus and Adonis*," ShS 15 (1962), 62–72.

of the crowd; for me may golden Apollo minister full cups from the Castalian fount"). Shakespeare, to Greene's disgust, had already demonstrated his capacity to "excite the marvel of the crowd," and was now set to challenge the University Wits on their own social and literary ground with an Ovidian poem that would be learned and copious, erotically and rhetorically sophisticated. From readers who knew their Ovid he might hope for recognition of the precise context of his quotation: concluding the first book of the *Amores*, the Latin poet defies "biting envy" and proclaims the immortality of poetry with a list that includes Homer, Hesiod, Sophocles, Menander, Virgil, Lucretius and Tibullus. Shakespeare, by recalling that context, lays implicit claim to the same distinguished ancestry; but transmitted to him, as it were, by a single mediator, the most protean of poets and the master of many moods.

Everything suggests a carefully calculated career-move. The printer was Richard Field, a Stratford fellow-citizen, who had brought out an impressive edition of the *Metamorphoses* in 1589. The dedicatee is the young Henry Wriothesley, Earl of Southampton, a patron of poets and already a faintly sulfurous figure. Shakespeare may or may not have found the germ of a recalcitrant Adonis in Southampton's aversion to marriage with Lord Burghley's granddaughter, Lady Elizabeth Vere.[2] The poem obviously develops in a way that leaves any such occasion far behind, but one need only think of the way Sidney teases his readers with hints of the "real story" behind *Astrophil and Stella* to see that the

---

[2] In 1591 John Clapham, one of Burghley's secretaries, had addressed to Southampton a moralistic Latin poem entitled *Narcissus*, and Shakespeare's Venus, in her turn, uses the example of Narcissus to warn Adonis against the dangers of self-love (157–62). Self-love, however, seems to be the only link between the chaste Adonis and the promiscuous Southampton. See Charles Martindale and Colin Burrow, "Clapham's *Narcissus*: A Pre-Text for Shakespeare's *Venus and Adonis* (text, translation, commentary)," *ELR* 22 (1992), 147–75. On the more general issue of Southampton's relations with Shakespeare see G. P. V. Akrigg, *Shakespeare and the Earl of Southampton* (London, 1968).

whiff of scandal would have done no harm to the popularity of *Venus and Adonis*. Taken together, the epigraph and the dedication steer a prudent middle course between self-advertisement and humility, making an ambitious claim to the inheritance of Ovid and at the same time demanding indulgence for "unpolished lines." The relation between poet and patron is given a conventionally feudal coloring with Southampton as the lord who stands "godfather" to the "first heir" of his vassal. Shakespeare, as one of the new and socially insecure class of professional writers, is making a discreet but unequivocal plea for admission to the court circle which was the source of patronage and the arbiter of literary reputation.

Shakespeare would have had no reason to be dissatisfied with his success. With ten printings during the poet's lifetime (more than for any of the plays), *Venus and Adonis* became a byword or touchstone for the kind of witty and erotic Ovidian narrative that went on to flourish well into the seventeenth century.[3] Indeed, with the possible exception of *The Faerie Queene*, it may be doubted whether any other poem of the period was quite so widely read.[4] It then practically disappeared from circulation for about a hundred and fifty years and neither the bardolatry of the nineteenth century nor the massive critical industry of our own times has been able to grant it much more than a marginal place in the Shakespearean canon. Even Coleridge's powerful advocacy was probably in the long run counter-productive insofar as he was more concerned to find evidence of Shakespeare's nascent poetic

---

[3] The standard anthology is *Elizabethan Minor Epics*, ed. Elizabeth Story Donno (New York, 1963) which begins with Thomas Lodge, *Scillaes Metamorphosis* (1589), and ends with James Shirley, *Narcissus or The Self-Lover* (1646).

[4] For "The Vogue of *Venus and Adonis* and *Lucrece*" see Rollins, 447–75. See also Katherine Duncan-Jones, "Much Ado with Red and White: The Earliest Readers of Shakespeare's *Venus and Adonis* (1593)," *RES* New Series XLIV, No. 176 (1993), 480–501. This is a fascinating and witty account of the "open responsiveness" of the poem's first readers, beginning with the eccentric William Reynolds who saw Venus as Queen Elizabeth and Adonis as himself.

powers than to make sense of the poem as a whole. He offers some brilliantly suggestive comment on specific passages such as the flight of Adonis in the dusk and he celebrates, as critics have done ever since, "the affectionate love of nature and natural objects" and the skill in painting "the very minutest beauties of the external world;"[5] but this emphasis on details of imagery could only encourage what became the standard Victorian view of the poem as essentially apprentice work, a mass of unrefined ore from which a few shining nuggets might be extracted by the discerning reader. In recent years *Venus and Adonis* has attracted substantial and appreciative attention from William Keach, Richard Lanham, Coppelia Kahn, Heather Dubrow and Jonathan Bate, but even as late as 1986, in a book that is otherwise almost painfully fashionable, we can still find Gary Waller complaining that the poem is too static, "with just too much argument and insufficient flowing sensuality to make it pleasurable reading."[6]

The initial obstacle to any appreciation of what *Venus and Adonis* has to offer is the sheer magnitude of Shakespeare's reputation. Is this a minor poem that would scarcely merit our attention if it were not by Shakespeare? Or is it a work that we would regard far more highly if it happened to be by someone else? The fact is that we simply cannot put ourselves back in 1593 and read the text without an awareness of Shakespeare's subsequent achievement. The continuities between the narrative poem and the *Sonnets* have long been recognized and go far beyond the common presence of a lovely boy or the shared arguments for procreation.[7] Nor would one want to deny that the confusion of gender roles in the poem prefigures, in a different key, the exploitation

---

[5] *Coleridge's Shakespearean Criticism*, ed. T. M. Raysor, 2 vols. (London, 1960), 1. 188–93 (p. 188).

[6] Gary Waller, *English Poetry in the Sixteenth Century* (London, 1986), 217.

[7] The most stimulating discussion of the continuities between the narrative poems and the *Sonnets* is in Heather Dubrow, *Captive Victors: Shakespeare's Narrative Poems and Sonnets* (Ithaca, NY, 1987).

of crossdressing and sexual ambivalence in the comedies. There is, however, a danger that we shall end up by seeing these continuities as more interesting than the poem itself. On the one hand, the poem is subtly diminished if we approach it with expectations created by the dramatist or the sonneteer: on the other hand, not much is to be gained by such an inversion of the process as the eccentric attempt of Ted Hughes to make *Venus and Adonis* the mythological key that unlocks the whole of Shakespeare.[8] To accept the complete Shakespeare as a relevant and inevitable context for interpretation need not become a pretext for neglecting to read the poem on its own terms as an accomplished and mature performance in a genre to which the poet never returned.

As a preliminary to any interpretation or commentary, it may be as well to clear the ground by looking at some of the common prejudices or misconceptions that have got in the poem's way. One of these derives, strangely enough, from the very fact of its initial success. For many readers, a cloud of suspicion must hang over a work that was apparently so deliberately designed to establish a literary reputation and to satisfy a specifically Elizabethan taste. Behind the repeated assertions that the poem is cold, unfeeling, a mere sideline, an exercise in convention or a self-conscious display of virtuosity lies the unmistakable implication that *Venus and Adonis* is not "the real Shakespeare," that the poet was working against his natural grain in a pardonable but misguided attempt to jump on the fashionable Ovidian bandwagon. This is, however, a rather unconvincing way of escaping from the challenge of a poem that is both obviously Shakespearean and rather unlike anything else by Shakespeare. Shakespeare certainly was making a bid for the kind of literary respectability that the theatre alone could not provide, but neither he nor any other Renaissance poet would have seen such a move as other than a perfectly normal and laudable

---

[8] Ted Hughes, *Shakespeare and the Goddess of Complete Being* (London, 1992).

professional ambition. Moreover, the whole idea of a Shakespeare momentarily seduced by the Ovidian fashion will not stand up to examination. As Jonathan Bate has demonstrated, Shakespeare's engagement with Ovid lasts throughout his career; it shows up not only in the proliferation of Ovidian allusions, but also in the extraordinary range of his empathy, in his awareness of the provisional and flexible nature of sexual identity, in all those qualities that Bate so aptly describes as "mercurial."[9] Shakespeare is so deeply Ovidian that there is no justification for regarding *Venus and Adonis* as an opportunistic response to some specifically Ovidian moment. Not without reason did Francis Meres see Shakespeare as the reincarnation of the "sweet witty soul of Ovid": Shakespeare at his most Ovidian is most emphatically himself.[10]

One may also question whether in the England of 1593 the Ovidian epyllion was really such a fashionable genre as literary history has led us to believe.[11] Shakespeare used Arthur Golding's influential translation of the *Metamorphoses* (1565–67) and he may possibly have been aware of such insignificant adaptations as the anonymous *Fable of Ovid treting of Narcissus* (1560) or Thomas Peend's *Pleasant fable of Salmacis and Hermaphroditus* (1565), but it takes a drastic foreshortening of literary history to see texts that were already twenty-five or thirty years old as constituting the fashion in the 1590s. Shakespeare may have heard of Marlowe's *Hero and Leander* which was entered in the Stationers' Register in the same year as *Venus and*

---

[9] Jonathan Bate, *Shakespeare and Ovid* (Oxford, 1993), 270.

[10] Francis Meres, *Palladis Tamia* (1598) in *Elizabethan Critical Essays* ed. G. Gregory Smith, 2 vols. (Oxford, 1904), ii. 317.

[11] "Epyllion" (little epic) is a convenient if anachronistic shorthand for the Ovidian erotic narrative poem. On the origins of the term see Walter Allen, Jr., "The Non-Existent Classical Epyllion," *SP* 55 (1958), 515–18. As my last chapter will suggest, I am tempted by the Italian *idillio*, but "idyll" would have inappropriate Tennysonian echoes.

Adonis; there is, however, no solid evidence that he was influenced by it.[12] This leaves us with Thomas Lodge's *Scillaes Metamorphosis* (1589) as the only notable English epyllion before *Venus and Adonis*. On the other hand, the rapid development of the epyllion after 1593 is clearly marked by Shakespeare's example and the basic situation of sexually aggressive female and reluctant or inexperienced youth recurs in such poems as Michael Drayton's *Endimion and Phoebe* (1595), Francis Beaumont's *Salmacis and Hermaphroditus* (1602) and Phineas Fletcher's *Venus and Anchises* (1628). In this light *Venus and Adonis* appears less as an exercise in a conventional genre than as one of the two or three poems that promoted the genre and created its characteristic themes and manner. Shakespeare, on this occasion, did more than jump on a bandwagon; he set the wagon rolling.

More serious than the prejudice against *Venus and Adonis* as a concession to fashionable taste is the objection that it fails to establish any consistent atmosphere and lacks any unifying intention. C. S. Lewis' remark that "as we read on we become more and more doubtful how the work should be taken" is, at least, a comprehensible reaction to the poem's rapid and disturbing shifts in tone.[13] Sexual desire is represented both with highflown Petrarchan imagery and in terms of earthy physicality; Venus is both the grotesquely large and smothering female who can tuck Adonis under her arm and the lightfooted goddess whose passage leaves no trace in the sand; Adonis appears now as a petulant self-obsessed adolescent and now as an innocent victim of attempted rape before emerging in his final speech as a spokesman for

---

[12] We have ample evidence that *Hero and Leander* was widely read before its earliest extant edition in 1598. It may seem to echo or foreshadow Shakespeare by presenting Adonis as "careless and disdainful" (l. 13) and by describing him as "rose-cheeked" (l. 93); but there is nothing here that need strain our belief in coincidence.

[13] C. S. Lewis, *English Literature in the Sixteenth Century, Excluding Drama* (London, 1954), 498.

ideal love; the narrator may express his sympathy with one protagonist or the other and then distance himself in a way that accounts for Coleridge's comment on "the utter aloofness of the poet's own feelings from those of which he is at once the painter and the analyst."[14] At times the poem seems to nudge us towards an allegory of Lust and Chastity or Love and Death and then again we are brought back to an ironic psychological comedy where such large abstractions appear remote if not quite irrelevant. And no sooner have we opted for comedy than we are threatened with a flood of pathos. Unable or unwilling to cope with this bewildering display of legerdemain, Lewis concludes that *Venus and Adonis* falls between two stools, being neither genuinely erotic in its presentation of the sexual appetite nor clearly didactic as a warning against lust.

Lewis may have an unduly sanitized view of what constitutes the erotic (he cannot forgive Shakespeare for making Venus sweat), but he does have the real merit of recognizing that the poem cannot be read either as a coherent moral allegory or as straightforward eroticism. Too many attempts to rescue the reputation of *Venus and Adonis* have ended with interpretations that fail to acknowledge the elements that generate Lewis' perplexed reaction. To take one extreme tendency, attempts to read the poem in the light of *Ovide moralisé* obviously fall apart. Both *Ovide moralisé* and Golding see the fate of Adonis as illustrating what happens to a young man who gives way to lust; but it is hard to see what moral lesson is being taught by Shakespeare's version where Adonis resists the advances of Venus and gets killed just the same. Can we, instead, see the poem as a simple story of offended innocence with Venus, like Tarquin, as a figure of destructive lust and Adonis, like Lucrece, as a martyr of chastity or reason in love?[15]

---

[14] S. T. Coleridge, *Biographia Literaria*, 2 vols., ed. J. Shawcross (London, 1954), ii. 15–16.

[15] "Venus is shown as the destructive agent of sensual love; Adonis as reason in love. The one sullies whatever it touches: the other honors and makes it beautiful.

Shakespeare's sullen youth seems an unlikely candidate for canonization and his Venus can be tender as well as aggressive; but the real problem with such readings is that they depend so heavily on the idea that the boar is "Venus in her most horrible symbol."[16] Venus has, in fact, warned Adonis against the boar and it is a pretty confused allegory that asks us to hold her responsible for the destructive act that she has done everything to prevent.

Rather more promising in that it accounts for the narrator's blend of balanced sympathy and amused neutrality might be Donald Watson's argument that the poem is an unresolved debate between the Concupiscible (Venus) and the Irascible (Adonis) and that it is the failure to reconcile these opposed but necessary temperaments that provokes the final catastrophe. Adonis, however, is surely too self-controlled to represent the Irascible (compare Pyrochles in *Faerie Queene*, Book II), and it seems an unduly cerebral and flattening approach that sees Venus and Adonis "more as psychological dispositions than as dramatic characters"[17]. One suspects that any reading which needs to call on Aristotle, Augustine and Aquinas has become rather remote from the book that the undergraduate Gullio placed under his pillow and from the "luscious marrow-bone pie" that Middleton's Harebrain feared might corrupt his bride.[18] It is not that allegory and eroticism are mutually exclusive but that the eroticism of *Venus and Adonis* simply does not raise—except, as we shall see, in a

---

The one is false and evil; the other is all truth, all good. [...] This is the teaching of *Venus and Adonis*, as didactic a piece of work, perhaps, as Shakespeare ever wrote." L. E. Pearson, *Elizabethan Love Conventions* (New York, 1933), 285.

[16] Hereward T. Price, "The Function of Imagery in *Venus and Adonis*," *Papers of the Michigan Academy of Science, Arts and Letters* 31 (1945), 275–97 (p. 292).

[17] Donald G. Watson, "The Contrarieties of *Venus and Adonis*," *SP* 75 (1978), 32–63 (p. 54).

[18] *The Return from Parnassus, Part I* (1600); Thomas Middleton, *A Mad World, my Masters* (1608). Both cited in Rollins, 455.

provisional and ironic fashion—the kind of issues that allegory is equipped to handle. The depth of the poem is not philosophical or theological and the subtlety of its sexual psychology goes well beyond anything that can be expressed in terms of conventional Renaissance "dispositions." It is, after all, a characteristic of the Ovidian epyllion and a probable cause of its popularity that, by its recourse to stories that combined the dignity of classical ancestry with the license granted to entertaining fables, it allowed not just eroticism but also a more free, dispassionate and investigative approach to sexuality than was possible in official discourse on the topic. When Gary Waller objects that *Venus and Adonis* relies too much "upon heavy moralizing allegory" one suspects that he has been reading not the poem itself but some of the many critical attempts to reduce its content to the platitudes of Renaissance orthodoxy.[19]

The most seductive allegorical readings are probably those that look to Neoplatonism. Since the days of Kristeller, Gombrich and Wind we have grown less inclined to see Neoplatonism as the dominant current in Renaissance thought as a whole, but it was certainly a pervasive element in the sixteenth-century rhetoric of love. Its total absence would be surprising in a poem where rhetoric turns out to be a central issue. T. W. Baldwin brings massive erudition to support his claim that "the argument of *Venus and Adonis* is all worked through in proper Platonic order to a proper Platonic conclusion, as interpreted by Ficino and his followers"—which turns out to mean that Adonis is "Beauty or true Love refusing to be won by Venus-Lust to propagation."[20] And yet, though the Neoplatonic echoes that Baldwin documents so thoroughly can hardly be denied, this reading takes little account of the problematic context in which they are placed by

---

[19] Waller, 217.

[20] T. W. Baldwin, *On the Literary Genetics of Shakspere's Poems and Sonnets* (Urbana, Ill., 1943), 83–84.

Shakespeare's characterization of Adonis. To make Adonis an embodiment of true love rather than of chastity involves taking his final speech (769–810) at its face value and it still leaves us with an ideal figure that we fail to recognize in the complex (and complexed) youth of the text. Using Neoplatonism to redeem Venus, Heather Asals sees in her development from comedy to pathos a version of the ascension from sensual love to the contemplation of pure beauty and truth that we find in the treatises of Ficino, Bembo and Castiglione;[21] but this "education of a goddess" is no more convincing than the ideal Adonis. Though there certainly is a difference between the sexually aggressive Venus of the opening and the mourning maternal Venus of the end, it is by no means clear that the poem invites us to see this change as progress from a lower to a higher stage. Venus' repeated claims that Adonis embodies the ideal beauty towards which nature strives or the source of harmony without which the world will return to chaos (11–12, 727–32, 953–54, 1015–20, 1079–80) may suggest a Neoplatonic program, but they are constantly undermined by her own demands for immediate physical satisfaction. For her, as for Sidney's Astrophil, "Desire still cries, give me some food" (*Astrophil and Stella*, 71). When she complains that the death of Adonis has deprived the world of a prelapsarian harmony or of "true sweet beauty" (1080), the reader cannot be sure whether to take this as the final recognition of a Neoplatonic ideal or as a vindictive hyperbole designed to justify the curse on love that will follow. Nor can we think of Venus as having achieved any culminating vision of the truth when her own account of her relationship with Adonis (1069–1120, 1177–88) is so self-indulgently expurgated as to give no hint of her aggression or his resistance. The fact is that Shakespeare is careful to avoid any facile contrast between the old Venus and the new. There is no sense of conversion or enlightenment. It is, if anything, the continuities that are

---

[21] Heather Asals, "*Venus and Adonis*: The Education of a Goddess," *SEL* 13 (1973), 31–51.

striking. Her desire for Adonis has, from the start, co-existed with maternal protective elements and her transformation into a *mater dolorosa* remains erotic. The final incestuous image of the Adonis-flower as a son who takes his father's place in the mother's bed is a fitting conclusion to the story of a passion where the erotic and the maternal are so intricately woven that the movement from one to the other must be seen less as an ascent than as a shift of emphasis.

More circumspectly, Lennet Daigle argues that *Venus and Adonis* confronts two systems of value. In one of these Venus stands condemned as the personification of lust; in the other she is the Neoplatonic heavenly goddess who, as the source of generation (Venus Genitrix), ensures the continuation of a divinely established order of nature. It is, he believes, in the latter terms that the poem finally vindicates the demands of Venus.[22] This, however, begs more questions than it answers. Why, if she is to be seen as the beneficent patroness of a natural order, does she end by placing a curse on all future lovers? Why does she depart and leave the world to its own devices? How seriously are we supposed to take arguments for procreation that are the traditional stock-in-trade of seducers? John Roe comes much nearer to defining the role of Neoplatonism in *Venus and Adonis* when he remarks that "the Neoplatonic vision, which is glimpsed sporadically and, in the main, comically earlier in the poem, functions seriously at the close not as its own triumphant principle but as an enhancement of tragic pathos."[23] One would only want to add that even at the close the pathos generated by that Neoplatonic vision is still veined with the irony that one would expect in a poem where Neoplatonism is viewed critically as one source of a rhetoric that is always in excess of or inadequate to the reality of a sexual situation.

---

[22] Lennet J. Daigle, "*Venus and Adonis*: Some Traditional Contexts," *Shakespeare Studies* 13 (1980), 31–46.

[23] Roe, 21.

For a robust counter to the solemnities of allegory and a release from Lewis' erotic-didactic dilemma, we might turn to Rufus Putney who stresses the poem's comic dimension to the exclusion of almost everything else.[24] Unfortunately, Putney's approach is woefully heavy-handed. He underestimates the pathos and the psychological insight that prevent the poem from becoming a Renaissance version of Fielding's Lady Booby and Joseph Andrews; his useful recognition that the rhetoric is sometimes parodic is vitiated by his tendency to reduce the whole issue of rhetoric to mere debunking. His frequent recourse to the term "farce" should warn us that he has lost sight of the sophisticated erotic comedy that the Elizabethans enjoyed. Eroticism and comedy are perfectly compatible; eroticism and farce are certainly not. There may be passages when the poem does, indeed, teeter on the edge of slapstick ("He on her belly falls, she on her back," 594), but it is worth noting how rapidly Shakespeare draws back from the brink as if he is repeatedly trying to test how far he can push the extremes of comedy and pathos without breaking the link between them. That kind of tension is as absent from Putney's reading as it is from the straitjackets of the allegory-mongers.

In the long run, most of the debate about "how the work should be taken" boils down to the central issue of its flamboyant rhetoric. Lewis' failure to appreciate *Venus and Adonis* may be traced back to his conviction that "rhetoric is the greatest barrier between us and our ancestors"[25] and Douglas Bush takes a similar line when, in extenuation of a text where "action bears to rhetoric much the same proportion as bread to sack in Falstaff's bill," he pleads that "the conceited style was instinctive with most Elizabethans as it cannot be with us." Like Victorian readers of the poem, Bush insists that

---

[24] Rufus Putney, "*Venus and Adonis*: Amour with Humor," *PQ* 20 (1941), 533–48; "Venus Agonistes," *University of Colorado Studies* 4 (1953), 52–66.

[25] Lewis, 61.

"Shakespeare's best bits of imagery are fresh pictures of nature," but neither these crumbs of comfort nor his grudging admiration for the rhetoric's "inexhaustible energy" are enough to save a "soulless" poem where the occasional flashes of "truth and actuality" only draw attention to the bookish artificiality of the rest.[26]

The fact is that Bush and Lewis, with all their feeling for Renaissance poetry, still inherit the Romantic distrust of rhetoric that we find so vigorously expressed in Hazlitt's essay of 1817:

> The two poems of Venus and Adonis and of Tarquin and Lucrece appear to us like a couple of ice-houses. They are about as hard, as glittering, and as cold. The author seems all the time to be thinking of his verses, and not of his subject,—not of what his characters would feel, but of what he shall say; and as it must happen in all such cases, he always puts into their mouths those things which they would be the last to think of, and which it shows the greatest ingenuity in him to find out. The whole is laboured, up-hill work. The poet is perpetually singling out the difficulties of the art to make an exhibition of his strength and skill in wrestling with them. He is making perpetual trials of them as if his mastery over them were doubted. The images, which are often striking, are generally applied to things which they are the least like: so that they do not blend with the poem, but seem stuck upon it, like splendid patchwork, or remain quite distinct from it, like detached substances, painted and varnished over. A beautiful thought is bound to be lost in an endless commentary upon it. The speakers are like persons who have both leisure and inclination to make riddles on their own situation, and to twist and turn every object or incident into acrostics or anagrams. Everything is spun out into an allegory; and a digression is always preferred to the main story. Sentiment is built up upon plays of words; the hero or heroine feels, not from the impulse of passion, but from the force of dialectics.[27]

---

[26] Douglas Bush, *Mythology and the Renaissance Tradition in English Poetry* (1932, rev. edn., New York, 1963), 137–55.

[27] William Hazlitt, *Characters of Shakespeare's Plays* (London, 1906), 264–65.

The attack on Shakespeare's rhetoric is mounted with formidable rhetorical energy. Hazlitt, like Dr. Johnson, has the capacity to force one's admiration at the very moment when he provokes the strongest disagreement. He puts his finger unerringly upon the basic problem by recognizing that rhetorical display is central to the way the narrative poems function. If we cannot come to terms with that display, then no amount of striking imagery will serve to acquit *Venus and Adonis* of being "splendid patch-work." Where Bush and others have seen the rhetoric as the "instinctive" linguistic excess of a young Elizabethan, Hazlitt's comment that the poet singles out and wrestles with "the difficulties of the art" points to the way the poem deliberately highlights rhetoric as a problem. If "a digression is always preferred to the main story," it may well be that the main story is, in some sense, unspeakable. It will not do to see the rhetoric as a husk to be peeled away in order to get at the poem's kernel. The statement that "sentiment is built up upon plays of words" and that the protagonists feel "from the force of dialectics" may be taken without the irony that Hazlitt intended. Venus and Adonis exist in and not behind their rhetoric as surely as the characters of an opera exist in and not behind their music.

To understand the way rhetoric works in *Venus and Adonis* we need to start from Shakespeare's crucial modification of the Ovidian story (*Met,* X. 519–59, 705–39). In Ovid there is no suggestion that Adonis resists Venus or that the goddess has to resort to any extraordinary eloquence. For the Adonis of Ovid and of all sixteenth-century versions of the myth apart from Shakespeare's, Venus' own physical attractions are a more than sufficient argument. It is through his creation of an Adonis who resists that Shakespeare compensates for the myth's lack of action by turning the poem into a debate, thus restoring rhetoric to its primary function as persuasion. This is surely the major reason why the rhetoric of Venus does not pall like the rhetoric of Lucrece. When F. T. Prince remarks that "the greatest weakness of Shakespeare's Lucrece is her remorseless eloquence"[28] we might be tempted to say the same of Venus; but there is an essential difference. The eloquence of Lucrece, after a dozen stanzas of pleading with Tarquin, expands into an interminable post-rape soliloquy; the eloquence of Venus, for two thirds of the poem, is addressed to an antagonist and is, therefore, public in the sense of being geared to an audience within the text. Here, indeed, lies part of the answer to Hazlitt's objection that Shakespeare is always "thinking of his verses" and "not of what his characters would feel." Venus and Adonis do not primarily speak in order to express their feelings, but in order to win an argument which has immediate and practical consequences. They are, that is to say, in an essentially rhetorical situation. It is not that Shakespeare is uninterested in what his characters feel or that he reduces them to mere vehicles of the conventional arguments for and against sexual intercourse. The feelings emerge, as it were, through the shadings and interstices of the rhetoric, through incomplete analogies, metaphors that fail to fit the case, gaps in the argument, contradictions and changes in strategy. Venus and Adonis fall into what might be called the double trap of rhetoric which controls the speaker who thinks it can be neglected and betrays the speaker who tries to exploit it, revealing something more or other than was intended. Thus, to take only a few examples that will be discussed more fully later on, Venus cannot argue that Adonis should take the male initiative without effectively appropriating the male role for herself; and her advocacy of procreation (in keeping with her mythical status as Venus Genitrix) fails to mask the underlying truth that one aspect of her passion is not to have a child by Adonis but to have Adonis as her child. Adonis seizes on this disjunction between motive and argument to condemn the rhetoric of Venus as both ineffective ("Your treatise makes me like you worse and worse," 774) and dishonest ("reason is the bawd to lust's abuse," 792), but lays himself open to the same accusations when he

---

[28] Prince, xxxvi.

embarks on a series of conventional and aphoristic distinctions between lust and love that have nothing to do with his own need "to grow unto himself" (1180) or with his crippling fear of sexual experience as something that would damage his fragile and immature sense of autonomy.

It is, therefore, a basic mistake to think of *Venus and Adonis* as a poem where Shakespeare or his characters indulge in rhetoric as an end in itself. Venus may derive some wry satisfaction from her own rhetorical skills, but there is no justification for Tita French Baumlin's insistence on seeing Venus as a budding poet, a figure for the apprentice bard.[29] The fact that Venus (like so many Shakespearean characters) uses rhetoric in a self-conscious fashion need not mean that rhetorical brilliance is her main preoccupation. Shakespeare himself is undoubtedly concerned with the nature of rhetoric, but one may doubt whether he would even have understood a concept like "rhetoric as an end in itself." What matters to him in *Venus and Adonis* is rhetoric as functional and dysfunctional, the ways in which it succeeds or fails in producing a concrete result. Richard Lanham's observation that "far from being infatuated with rhetoric, he fashions a mature satire in which it becomes the principal target"[30] is perceptive enough, but could be misleading if it leads us to think that *Venus and Adonis* takes a straightforwardly anti-rhetorical stance. The satire is "mature" precisely because the poem accepts rhetoric as inevitable and demonstrates both its power and its limits. To grasp this one need only look at Venus' plea for procreation as the "law of nature" (171) or at Adonis' reply that sexual initiation should wait upon ripeness and self-knowledge (415–20, 523–28). Both arguments are advanced with

---

[29] Tita French Baumlin, "The Birth of the Bard: *Venus and Adonis* and Poetic Apotheosis," *Southern Illinois Papers on Language and Literature* 26 (1990), 191–211.

[30] Richard Lanham, *The Motives of Eloquence: Literary Rhetoric in the Renaissance* (New Haven, Conn., 1976), 90.

considerable rhetorical efficiency and the reader surely realizes that they are not, in the long run, irreconcilable. That Venus is more interested in copulation than in procreation or that Adonis is only looking for a pretext to get off the hook may indeed underline their rhetorical dexterity in finding arguments to suit their respective predicaments. The gap between underlying motive and explicit argument makes the rhetoric ineffective for its audience within the poem (its addressee) without totally undermining its effect on the audience outside the poem. We are led to a heightened awareness that the efficacy of rhetoric depends upon context and that it is perfectly possible for rhetoric to exist in two contexts at the same time. The reader, whatever his instinctive sympathies, can hardly avoid comparing his own reactions with those of the poem's protagonists and he is free to find the rhetoric of Venus highly persuasive while recognizing that it is inappropriate for persuading Adonis.

Venus and Adonis is a poem that draws our attention to the complex implications of the Renaissance obsession with rhetoric. Seen from one angle, Renaissance rhetoric functions as an instrument of social control. With its listing of tropes and figures from *ablatio* to *zeugma*, it seems to impose order on the chaos of language; with its emphasis on decorum and levels of discourse, it reinforces hierarchical divisions; as the basis of a humanist education, it is a competence that distinguishes the rulers from the ruled. Seen from another angle, the centrality of rhetoric may appear as potentially subversive. To be trained to argue *in utramque partem*, to regard arguments in terms of their immediate effectiveness rather than their abstract validity, to cultivate the skills of the debater rather than those of the logician—all these aspects of a rhetorical education might encourage a relativist outlook that would place any orthodoxy at risk. It is in this light that we can look yet again at the "law of nature" which provides Venus with her basic arguments. Natural analogies always come in handy for ideologies which seek to appear as the reflection of some timeless order; but, as David Norbrook points out, by the sixteenth century natural analogies in political discourse were increasingly "attended with an awareness that they were rhetorical constructs with evident palpable designs on their audience."[31] The same is obviously true of sexual discourse in *Venus and Adonis*—not only because Venus uses natural analogies with a literally "palpable" end in view, but because the analogies themselves (the natural behavior of the horses, the ripe fruit that must be plucked) turn out to be double-edged. When Adonis also appeals to nature, the text surely invites the "resisting reader" (Norbrook's phrase) to conclude that the natural analogies in which rhetoric delights can be used to justify more or less anything. That the poem's most elaborate rhetoric should be uttered by a woman (even one who is a goddess) is also, of course, potentially subversive. How are we to distinguish between the *copia* that is the result of the male's rhetorical training and the garrulity which is a traditional mark of female inferiority? Is the practice of rhetoric diminished when it can be "mastered" by a woman or is the woman revalued by her demonstration of competence in a supposedly male domain?

However ethically dubious we may find the practice of rhetoric, it remains necessary in a fallen world if only because it can achieve practical results where purely rational arguments are likely to fail. It is, however, a powerful instrument rather than a precision tool and its functioning is anything but automatic. Venus, in the course of the poem, moves from a situation where she uses rhetoric in traditional humanist fashion as a means of persuasion to one where, after the death of Adonis, it becomes a way of reinventing experience. As she does so, she discovers to her cost that rhetoric can neither guarantee desired results in a real world nor detach itself from experience to create a world of its own. To become embroiled in the indirections and approximations of rhetoric is part of the penalty that a goddess pays for descending to a human condition.

---

[31] David Norbrook, "Rhetoric, Ideology and the Elizabethan World Picture," in *Renaissance Rhetoric*, ed. Peter Mack (London, 1994), 140–64 (p. 147).

If the barrier of the poem's rhetoric dissolves as soon as we see that rhetoric itself is being subjected to a witty and critical appraisal, the same can be said of the poem's approach to myth. What myth and rhetoric have in common is that, while we seem unable to speak of ourselves without them, there is no myth and no rhetoric that is ever perfectly adapted to a specific human situation. *Venus and Adonis* investigates the functions and dysfunctions of rhetoric; it also investigates the relevance and irrelevance of myth.

It should hardly be necessary to demonstrate that Shakespeare, unlike the Spenser of *Faerie Queene*, Book III, has little interest in exploiting the story of Venus and Adonis as a cosmic or vegetative myth. Venus, when it serves her own interests, may assume the traits of Venus Genitrix, but Adonis bears no relation to the "Father of all forms," and the ending of the poem, as I shall argue in Chapter Four, seems expressly designed to defeat any hope of rebirth or any attempt to see Adonis as the sacrificial young victim whose blood regenerates the world. The Venus who makes her body into a deer-park (229–40) and who addresses Adonis as an "earthly sun" (198) certainly recalls the tradition that reads Venus as the upper hemisphere of the earth, Adonis as the sun and the boar as winter,[32] but these allusions serve more as an ironic counterpoint to the theme of frustrated copulation than as a recognition that the protagonists have a truly mythical dimension. Must we, therefore, assume that Shakespeare is using the myth only as a pretext for what turns out to be a very human drama? It is, no doubt, very tempting to see Venus as "a forty-year-old countess

---

[32] See Abraham Fraunce, *The Third part of the Countess of Pembrokes Yvychurch* (London, 1592). The cosmological reading of the myth was a Renaissance commonplace which Fraunce could have picked up from Boccaccio's *Genealogia Deorum* or from a number of popular manuals such as those of Natalis Comes (1551) and Vincenzo Cartari (1556) or, in England, Thomas Cooper (1565).

with a taste for Chapel Royal altos"[33] or as a sixteenth-century Erica Jong for whom "feisty" would be the only appropriate adjective. The problem is that Shakespeare does not allow us to forget that Venus is, after all, a goddess. The narrator is usually careful to acknowledge her regal title and even Adonis, in a rare moment of courtesy, addresses her as "Fair queen" (523). Venus herself is highly conscious of her own divinity, reminding Adonis that she is immortal ("And were I not immortal, life were done," 197), that she is perennially youthful ("My beauty as the spring doth yearly grow," 141) and that, despite his experience of her weight, she can defy the laws of gravity ("Two strengthless doves will draw me through the sky," 153). Thus we are repeatedly made aware of the gap between Venus' status as the goddess of love and the all-too-human condition to which she has been reduced by Adonis' resistance. The narrator stresses the point with pungent formulae ("Being judge in love, she cannot right her cause," 220; "Poor queen of love, in thine own law forlorn," 251), and it is not only the reader but Venus herself who discovers that on this occasion the goddess can no longer perform the role assigned to her by the mythographers. *Venus and Adonis* is not simply a poem about a mature woman's frustrated desire for a younger man; it is also and equally a poem about a goddess who finds out what it is like to be human.

Among the many things that must have struck Shakespeare in his reading of Ovid is the fact that when the gods are seized with desire for mortals the first casualty is usually their own dignity: *non bene conveniunt nec in una sede morantur / maiestas et amor* ("Majesty and love do not go well together, nor tarry long in the same dwelling place," *Met*, II. 846–47). In Book VI of the *Metamorphoses* the weaving contest between Minerva and Arachne offers two sharply contrasting pictures of the relations between the Olympians and their

---

[33] Don Cameron Allen, "On *Venus and Adonis*," in *Elizabethan and Jacobean Studies Presented to F. P. Wilson*, ed. H. Davis and H. Gardner (Oxford, 1959), 100–11 (p. 101).

human subjects. Minerva predictably portrays the heavenly gods in statuesque poses, decked with the emblems of their authority as the guardians of law and order: in the four corners of her tapestry audacious mortals are punished for their presumption with a variety of unpleasant metamorphoses. Arachne also portrays metamorphoses, but now at the center of the web. And they are those in which the gods themselves, no longer awesome and statuesque, indulge to seduce innocent mortal women—Jove as a bull, an eagle or a swan, Neptune as a ram or a dolphin, Phoebus as a hawk and Saturn as a horse. Ovid makes it clear that Arachne does not lose the contest; she is, indeed, only too successful:

> Non illud Pallas, non illud carpere Livor
> possit opus: doluit successu flava virago
> et rupit pictas, caelestia crimina, vestes.
> (*Met*, VI. 129–31)

> Not Pallas, nor Envy himself, could find a flaw in that work. The golden-haired goddess was indignant at her success, and rent the embroidered web with its heavenly crimes.

What provokes Minerva's rage is not only Arachne's unsurpassable skill but the very subject-matter of her work which shows the gods as both criminal and comic, descending below the human into animal forms in order to satisfy their lusts. It is no wonder that Minerva, by transforming Arachne into a spider, condemns her to non-figurative art.[34]

Ovid's own poem (apart from the last book) takes a distinctly Arachnean line and for poets of Shakespeare's generation it was this irreverent and ironic portrayal of the gods, with its opportunities for

---

[34] For an illuminating discussion of the Arachne episode see the opening chapter of Leonard Barkan, *The Gods Made Flesh: Metamorphosis and the Pursuit of Paganism* (New Haven, Conn., 1986).

eroticism and comedy, that proved irresistible. Marlowe's *Hero and Leander* sets the tone when, in an ecphrasis that recalls Arachne's tapestry, it presents the pictures that adorn the pavement of the temple of Venus:

> There might you see the gods in sundry shapes
> Committing heady riots, incest, rapes:
> For know that underneath this radiant floor
> Was Danae's statue in a brazen tower,
> Jove slyly stealing from his sister's bed,
> To dally with Idalian Ganymede,
> Or for his love Europa bellowing loud,
> And tumbling with the Rainbow in a cloud.
> (*IIL*, I. 143–50)[35]

The self-inflicted indignity of Jove's behavior, neatly suggested by the verbs ("slyly stealing," "bellowing," "tumbling"), provides us with one set of expectations that Shakespeare's Venus will obviously fulfill. Reduced to blatant self-advertisement, sweating with passion and wrestling with Adonis, the ethereal goddess will be brought heavily down to earth.

There is, however, more to Ovid's presentation of the gods in love than mere ridicule and we should beware of adopting an approach that would lead us back to Putney's view of *Venus and Adonis* as unadulterated comedy. Ovid's humor is more subtle than broad and it is held in check by a recurrent vein of violence and terror. The behavior of the Olympians in Arachne's tapestry is, we are told, criminal; when a mortal virgin is chosen by a god, her sexual initiation usually takes the form of a rape. To the initial metamorphosis of the immortal aggressor corresponds the final metamorphosis of the mortal victim—as an

---

[35] Christopher Marlowe, *The Complete Poems and Translations*, ed. Stephen Orgel (Harmondsworth, 1971). All subsequent quotations of *Hero and Leander* are from this edition, followed by line reference in my text.

unjustified punishment (Juno's transformation of Callisto into a bear), as a strategy to avoid detection (Jupiter turning Io into a cow) or as an answer to the victim's own prayer (Daphne becoming a laurel to escape Apollo). This may sometimes function as an aesthetic solution that distances the real violence of the episode, but more often Ovid draws our attention to the pain involved in the gradual loss of human faculties and to the horror of imprisonment in a non-human shape. When the gods impose their lust on mortals they do more than violate the physical integrity of their victims; they end by depriving them of a recognizable human identity. Here then is another and darker aspect of Shakespeare's Ovidian inheritance. His violent Venus and virginal Adonis conform, at least in part, to the Ovidian pattern of lustful gods and innocent human victims. *Venus and Adonis* is Ovidian not least in the way it achieves a balance between the comedy and the terror of sexual initiation.

The complexity of Shakespeare's relation to Ovid can be seen in the fact that the direct source for his poem in the *Metamorphoses*, Book X, turns out to be an exception from the pattern described above. Ovid's Venus is, for a start, the only female divinity who descends to love a mortal and his Adonis is a willing partner rather than a victim. There is no animal disguise and no brutality; on the contrary, Venus does her best to please Adonis by adopting his way of life and accompanying him as a huntress, even if this means imitating the dress of her arch-rival Diana. The death of Adonis does not result from any divine vindictiveness and his metamorphosis is without pain. In this light it would seem that Shakespeare, by creating a more aggressive goddess, goes some way towards forcing Ovid's exception back into the more habitual Ovidian mold.

What we ultimately get in Shakespeare's poem is a version that stands midway between the dominant Ovidian pattern and what Ovid actually makes of the story of Venus and Adonis. The crucial factor is not simply that Adonis resists, but that his resistance is successful. Allowing for some important homosexual variations, the prevailing formula for Ovid's tales of gods and mortals can be presented schematically as follows: immortal, male, active, powerful vs mortal, female, passive, powerless. Shakespeare's startling and seminal innovation is to keep these attributes but reshuffle them so that we have a Venus who is immortal, female, active and powerless opposed to an Adonis who is mortal, male, passive and powerful. It is this redistribution that transforms the relation between divine and mortal into a real contest rather than a mere invasion and that creates in the reader a current of sympathy that can alternate between the two protagonists. Venus' demonstration of physical and rhetorical power is undermined by her biological status as a woman who cannot command Adonis' will—with all the sexual connotations that Shakespeare so often gives that term. Adonis, for all his mortal vulnerability and weakness, still has the power to withhold the one thing that Venus wants.

[For an immortal to be frustrated by a mortal is already a humiliation, but for the goddess of love the defeat is a more personal affront than it would be for any other Olympian. She fails in the very domain from which she takes her celestial title and prestige: "She's Love; she loves; and yet she is not loved" (610). The situation that seems on the surface so paradoxical can also be seen as perfectly logical: "Being judge in love, she cannot right her cause" (220). By falling in love with a mortal Venus momentarily loses her authority to control the loves of mortals; the judge has become a plaintiff.] From what we might call the Arachnean perspective the spectacle offers the acid satisfaction of seeing the biter bit. Ovid tells us that Adonis, in attracting the love of Venus, took revenge for his mother's fate (the incestuous passion of Myrrha),[36] and Shakespeare's narrator makes a similar point in more general fashion when he addresses Venus as "Poor queen of love, in thine own law forlorn" (251). The sympathetic

---

[36] *iam placet et Veneri matrisque ulciscitur ignes* (*Met*, X. 524).

tone is not without a touch of *Schadenfreude* as we are reminded that the goddess is now suffering the pains she habitually inflicts on others. Any reader of the *Metamorphoses* or the *Heroides* would know that Venus has rarely exercised her powers in a benevolent manner and would recognize in her final prophetic curse on lovers only a confirmation of the capricious way she has always behaved towards her unfortunate human subjects. Venus argues that because love has been bitter for her it will henceforth prove bitter for everyone else; the whole Ovidian tradition suggests that we should invert the proposition.

Despite the knowledge that we would expect her to have, Shakespeare's Venus seems to start with naively optimistic expectations of what love on earth should be. She encourages Adonis to accept his sexual initiation as the key to a new world of pleasure in a prelapsarian Eden "where never serpent hisses" (17) and as conformity with the "law of nature" that imposes procreation (171). On the one hand, by speaking of a "time-beguiling sport" (24), she suggests that lovemaking is an innocent pastime that Adonis need not take too seriously; on the other hand, she argues that it is man's most momentous activity as his only defense against mortality ("And so in spite of death thou dost survive," 173) and as a moral imperative ("Thou wast begot; to get it is thy duty," 168). What these two contrasting arguments have in common is that they both present love as an essentially unproblematic affair for which men require no guidance beyond that of their own natural inclinations ("For men will kiss even by their own direction," 216) and of nature itself. As Venus tells Adonis when she urges him to follow the example of his horse, the situation is so simple that words should not be needed.

> "Though I were dumb, yet his proceedings teach thee.
> O, learn to love! the lesson is but plain,
> And, once made perfect, never lost again."
> (406–08)

Unfortunately for the goddess, the lesson of nature is by no means as plain as she would like to believe. The horses communicate through an elaborate language of gesture that reflects more than it contradicts the conventions and complexities of human courtship (259–324). Moreover, if the horses do indeed follow the law of nature, then Venus has been the first to break that law by appropriating the male initiative. She loses on both counts: either the law of nature is not as simple as she assumes or she herself is responsible for creating an unnatural situation.

It is the complexities of Venus' own desire, her "variable passions" (967), that most radically undermine her plea for natural simplicity. If nature dictates mutual attraction between the sexes, what are we to make of the fact that Venus is attracted to Adonis by his feminine qualities ("Stain to all nymphs, more lovely than a man," 9)? If sexual intercourse is, as she argues, the fruit of maturity, how do we take her own admission that she wishes to taste Adonis while he is still "unripe" (127–28)? And, if it is an initiation into manhood, how does this fit with her repeated attempts to reduce him to the level of a child to be tempted with "honey secrets" and protected from the dangerous world by the playpen of a maternal body? Ambivalence reigns—nowhere more obviously than in the goddess's account of her affair with Mars (97–114) where what purports to be an invitation to imitate a virile conquest ends up as a demonstration of her own power to reduce the male to a state of unmanly and humiliating servitude.

Venus' profuse and ingenious rhetoric is not, therefore, just means in excess of matter. With all its elaborations, expansions, contradictions and shifts in strategy, it stands at odds with her basic argument that love is naturally simple. It gets her into a hole where she cannot stop digging. Through it she excites herself more than she excites Adonis and the result is a potentially endless rhythm of frustration where eloquence repeatedly topples over into physical aggression and where the defeat of that aggression provokes a new bout of eloquence. The physical entanglement of Adonis ("Look how a bird lies tangled in a net, / So fastened in her arms Adonis lies," 67–68) is analogous to the rhetorical entanglement of Venus herself. And Venus is entangled precisely because all her arguments in favor of simplicity keep revealing the complexity of motive which she cannot afford to acknowledge and from which she cannot escape.

The desire of Venus defies definition because it knows no limits. She sees Adonis not so much as a type who excites a specific kind of sexual appetite, but as an empty space, a blank page on which all forms of desire can be inscribed. Thus, by turns, she constructs him as an effeminate beauty who provides relief from male roughness, as a passive partner who allows her to assume the male role, as the virile rider who will manage her and take back that initiative for himself and as an eroticized child whose feeding (232–34) might grant her a variety of oral and incestuous satisfactions. Shakespeare's Venus unites in herself most of the varieties of desire that we find in the *Metamorphoses* where they proliferate to such an extent that we lose sight of any norm dictated by nature. Like Shakespeare's narrator who reproaches Venus for "Forgetting shame's pure blush and honor's wrack" (558), Ovid may at times throw up his hands in official horror and urge his chaste readers to proceed no further; but the overall direction of his poem is to challenge the idea that sexual desire has any preordained "natural" object. Desire in Ovid is naturally transgressive and this is surely part of the appeal of Renaissance Ovidian fictions in which, as Bruce Smith suggests, the reader "is invited, for a limited season, to give free play to desires that must ordinarily be held in check."[37] What we have already said of the poem's rhetoric is also true of its mythological content: both work against the idea of a normative nature.

It is, of course, entirely appropriate that the goddess of love should experience all those "variable passions" which assume the name of love. "She's Love; she loves," and it would be a limitation of her

---

[37] Bruce R. Smith, *Homosexual Desire in Shakespeare's England: A Cultural Poetics* (Chicago, 1991), 132.

divinity to restrict her to any single version of desire. "And yet she is not loved": it is the very range of her desires that prevents them from being realized in a specific and human sexual situation. Adonis is presented with lovemaking as an agreable pastime and also as a moral duty, urged to lie back and let it happen and then reproached for not taking the initiative, offered the female body as a safe haven from the dangerous world and also incited to possess it as a manly conquest. If the abundance of Venus' arguments reflects the range of her passions, then she must be truly insatiable since no single lover could respond to such multifarious demands. Readers who join too easily with Venus in condemning Adonis' refusal "To take advantage on presented joy" (405) underestimate the threat posed by the sheer profusion and incoherence of her persuasions. If Adonis replies "I know not love [. . .] nor will not know it" (409), this is partly because Venus has proved incapable of presenting love as something knowable. Love, in her rhetoric, is so riddled with contradictions as to justify Adonis' conclusion that it has no real substance: "For I have heard it is a life in death, / That laughs and weeps, and all but with a breath" (413–14). The love proposed by Venus appears so protean and so unstable, so much all and therefore nothing, that it can only threaten to dissolve rather than define the fragile identity of a youth who pleads "Before I know myself, seek not to know me" (525). Coppelia Kahn may be right to read *Venus and Adonis* as the story of a failed initiation, but the failure is not entirely to be blamed on Adonis.[38] Venus gives him every reason to believe that, in this case, carnal knowledge and self-knowledge are incompatible.

The opposition between the two protagonists is reinforced by a marked difference in rhetorical styles. The rhetoric of Venus is opportunistic and infinitely flexible, short on logic but strong on

---

[38] Coppelia Kahn, "Self and Eros in *Venus and Adonis*," *Centennial Review* 4 (1976), 351–71.

invention, expansive, all-embracing, taking whatever offers as grist to her mill. The flora and fauna inhabit her imagination, the landscape becomes her body, the sun participates in her inflamed passion and the behavior of the horses justifies her own sexual energy. Even when the death of Adonis finally destroys the illusion of a nature that mirrors and supports her intentions, the old habit dies hard and she makes a last desperate effort to read her own erotic motives into the mindless violence of the boar "Who did not whet his teeth at him again, / But by a kiss thought to persuade him there" (1113–14). Something of the same expansive quality can be observed in the mastery of tone that enables her to move from the seductive and the reassuring to the pathetic and the reproachful, or again in the astonishing variety of register that encompasses visionary Neoplatonism, sophisticated Petrarchism, libertine Ovidian wit and earthy sexual proverbs. She is, in short (or rather, at length), an anthology of love poetry.[39] Adonis speaks a good deal less—89 lines as against 384 for Venus in the debate that ends with his departure (811). He says enough, however, to embody a very different brand of rhetoric which, despite some revealing lapses into self-pity, is relatively even in tone, tightly organized, antithetical and aphoristic—the opposite of expansive, concerned with making rather than blurring distinctions.

> "Love comforteth, like sunshine after rain,
> But lust's effect is tempest after sun;
> Love's gentle spring doth always fresh remain;
> Lust's winter comes ere summer half be done:
>   Love surfeits not; lust like a glutton dies.
>   Love is all truth, lust full of forgèd lies."
> (799–804)

---

[39] Rob Maslen notes that "the language she uses is a giddyingly inventive display of familiar Petrarchan tropes," but this is a simplification. Petrarchism is only one ingredient in a very heady brew. See Rob Maslen, "*Venus and Adonis* and the Death of Orpheus," *Glasgow Review. Renaissance* 1 (1993), 70.

Critics have been quick to hear the voice of a diligent and priggish schoolboy reciting a well-learned lesson and there is certainly a hint of parody. But there is more to it than that. The clipped and rigorous symmetries of the syntax and the predictability of the antitheses convey Adonis' need to find security in a scheme of moral certainties, rigid boundaries and mutually absolute exclusions. The tidy, self-contained quality of the rhetoric is mimetic of his yearning for the "quiet closure" (782) and solitary "bedchamber" (784) where he can escape from the turbulent and chaotic emotions of Venus.

These two rhetorical styles can be seen as reflecting two opposed versions of the self. For Venus, with her blurring of distinctions, the self is asserted by reaching out to invade, incorporate and digest the world. For Adonis the self is created by the erection of barriers, by a refusal to let the world impinge on one's precious identity. We should, however, resist the temptation to oppose a Venus who is generous, creative, and life-enhancing to an Adonis who is selfish, sterile and life-denying. The truth is that both versions of the self are equally selfish and equally destructive of love. If Venus fails to persuade Adonis, it is because she refuses to recognize him as Other, because she cannot conceive of anything that resists absorption into the self. If Adonis cannot be persuaded, it is because he cannot conceive of the Other as anything but a threat to the self. Neither protagonist has any vision of the "mutual render" celebrated in the *Sonnets*, but they differ insofar as Adonis makes exclusion of the Other into a conscious principle whereas Venus seems quite unaware of the threat posed to Adonis by her own contrasting urge to absorb and incorporate. Thus she will, at times, use the metaphors of exchange, while instinctively developing them to suggest a very unequal bargain.[40] It is not just that the one kiss

---

[40] Dubrow (35–37) points out Venus' characteristic reliance on the conditional mode and relates it to her propensity for offering bargains where what is on offer is not something that Adonis wants. The same self-centredness is revealed by the rhetorical questions that assume answers Adonis would not in fact give.

she proposes to Adonis as the price of his freedom (84) soon becomes two thousand (522), but that who gives and who takes a kiss depends on context and perspective. "Take" can mean either "seize" or "accept;" "give" may be either "inflict" or "donate." Venus exploits the ambiguity of give and take in a way that is not so much dishonest as deeply self-regarding and pathetically self-deceptive.

That Venus should display this ignorance of her own motives is perfectly consistent with her status as a goddess. It is only humans who need to create and define an identity; the gods, immortal and immutable, are what they are. Since the identity of Venus as goddess of love is beyond question, self-knowledge is not her concern and she is, therefore, incapable of appreciating that concern in Adonis. Placed in a position where her biological status as woman prevents the automatic imposition of her will, she needs to persuade and she fails to grasp that persuasion cannot be effective without some recognition of the otherness of the addressee, of the obstinate selfhood that mortals hold so dear. Her rhetoric, after all, exemplifies the ambiguity of her status in the poem. In its profusion, exuberance and inventiveness, it is the reflection of her divinely creative powers as Venus Genitrix; in its confusions and revisions—or even by the simple fact that she needs rhetoric at all—it becomes the measure of her humiliation, a demonstration of how far she has fallen.

Venus sees no difference between lust and love; Adonis refuses to recognize the continuities between them.[41] Venus seeks to incorporate the world into the self; Adonis tries to construct a self in isolation from the world. Both the goddess who blurs all distinctions and the youth

---

[41] Catherine Belsey has noted that the narrator uses both "love" and "lust" as synonymous terms to indicate the passion of Venus. She argues that this reflects older attitudes, whereas Protestantism's positive revaluation of marriage created the need for rigid distinctions of the kind that Adonis makes at 793–804. Catherine Belsey, "Love as Trompe-l'oeil: Taxonomies of Desire in *Venus and Adonis*," *Shakespeare Quarterly* 40 (1995), 257–76.

who makes them hard and fast are victims of their own radical and self-centered simplification of experience. The poem does not adjudicate between them and neither does the boar. Readers who demand that the poem deliver a tidy moral package may see the boar as an embodiment of natural justice, punishing Venus for her destructive lust or Adonis for his self-imposed sterility; yet this is to miss the essential point that the boar represents not some offended natural law but nature's arbitrary violence. Though it is certainly in keeping with the theme of the poem that the death of Adonis should resemble a rape or a castration, the event in itself has no obvious or inevitable connection with Venus' desire or Adonis' resistance. To argue that Adonis is punished for not making love is much like saying that the victim of an aircrash has been punished for not staying at home. Venus herself, though she warns Adonis that hunting the boar is mortally dangerous, never suggests that death will be the punishment for his chastity. Her argument is only that, since accidents are always waiting to happen, Adonis should make love before death prevents him from doing so. Ovid's Adonis, we remember, does make love to Venus and gets killed just the same. For Shakespeare, as for Ovid, the death of Adonis remains an accident or, in the words of Venus, one of those "mad mischances" (738) which always lurk to "cross the curious workmanship of nature" (734).

As that line suggests, Venus fears the boar because his very existence gives the lie to her self-indulgent vision of a natural order that is in harmony with her own amorous and/or procreative inclinations: he represents that aspect of the world which stubbornly resists her rhetoric of incorporation. Already undermined by her own confused motives and challenged by Adonis' refusal to conform, her idea of the "law of nature" is finally destroyed by the boar's mindless brutality and by nature's manifest indifference to the beauty it produces but neglects to preserve. By descending to the human level Venus experiences both the human urge to discover order in the world and the world's resistance. Her reaction is a blend of impotence and vindictiveness. Reconstructing her own story as an etiological myth, she ordains that love shall henceforth be as unlucky for others as it has been for her (1135–64).

Imitating the boar who "would root these beauties as he roots the mead" (636), she deprives the world of the flower that is the last and only legacy of Adonis. It is not just Adonis but the world that has defeated her, and she leaves it in disgust.

I shall argue later that the poem's ending is not quite as depressing as this bald account makes it sound. The vindictiveness of Venus is balanced by her impotence. She leaves the world because she is obviously incapable of changing it—incapable not just of seducing Adonis but even of granting him the limited form of immortality that he receives in Ovid. Lovers need not fear the curses of a goddess who is so powerless. If the descent of Venus has not changed the world for the better, her departure will not make it any worse. We may, like Adonis, be the victims of nature's meaningless violence, but at least we shall not be the victims of the gods. Above all, the ending, with its goddess flying off into the sky and its youth transformed into a flower, reminds us that the myth, even in Shakespeare's untraditional version, has a partial and problematic relevance to any genuinely human situation. However convincingly Venus and Adonis may have acted human roles, they retain a fabulous dimension, existing outside history and outside society, abstracted in a theater of human passions without a human context. It is as if we have viewed ourselves not as we are in the world that is ours, but in a laboratory experiment through a glass that, because it enlarges and intensifies, also isolates and distorts. As mythical characters, Venus and Adonis are both like and unlike us—entangled in rhetoric as we all are and rhetorically constructed as the saner of us know that we are not. Coleridge remarked that *Venus and Adonis* seems "at once the characters themselves, but more, the representations of those characters by the most consummate actors."[42] Perhaps that is why, in the long run, we can contemplate the poem with

---

[42] *Shakespearean Criticism*, ii. 64.

the serenity that comes from an awareness that it illuminates but does not reproduce our own condition.

2

"The Heart's Attorney" Venus as Wooer

Few narrative poems pack so much into their opening lines as *Venus and Adonis*. As Coleridge remarked, "the whole stanza presents at once the time, the appearance of the morning, and the two persons distinctly characterized, and in six simple lines puts the reader in possession of the whole argument of the poem."[1] For a poem that has so often been condemned as both prolix and static, *Venus and Adonis* begins with surprising economy of means and with an extraordinary flurry of movement.

> Even as the sun with purple-coloured face
> Had ta'en his last leave of the weeping morn,
> Rose-cheeked Adonis hied him to the chase.
> Hunting he loved, but love he laughed to scorn.
>   Sick-thoughted Venus makes amain unto him,
>   And like a bold-faced suitor 'gins to woo him.
>   (1–6)

---

[1] *Shakespearean Criticism*, i. 192–93.

All the details combine to make the first stanza prefigure the whole poem. Allusions to the sun will recur at calculated intervals to establish a precise time-scheme[2] and the "purple-coloured face," besides suggesting the erotic heat of the encounter over which the sun presides, introduces one term in the binary color-scheme that will pervade the poem and conclude with "A purple flower sprung up, chequered with white" (1168). The implied comparison between Adonis and the sun (which Venus will render explicit, 197–98, 863–64) involves a subtle blend of similarity and difference: purple and rose, though close in the spectrum, are opposed in their respective connotations of inflamed passion and blushing innocence; the sun's leavetaking of the "weeping morn" at daybreak anticipates Adonis' departure from the weeping Venus at nightfall, but the sun will return and Adonis will not. The rhetorical neatness of "Hunting he loved, but love he laughed to scorn," with its polyptoton and paronomasia, prepares us for the clipped, self-sufficient and categorical quality that will be typical of Adonis when he speaks for himself, but it also initiates the poem's complex play of antithesis and analogy between hunting and love, and hints at the reversal by which the youth who loves to hunt will be hunted by love. Finally, as we move from the face of the sun and the cheeks of Adonis to the countenance of the goddess, an antithetical pair of compound adjectives, "sick-thoughted" and "bold-faced," warns us that the rhetoric of Venus, however superficially exuberant, will be generated more by anxiety than by self-confidence.

At a first reading it would look as if Shakespeare is following Horace's celebrated injunction to begin *in medias res*, but this turns out to be an illusion since that phrase only makes sense if the reader is, at some later stage, made conscious of the omitted antecedents. Thus

---

[2] For an elaborate but unconvincing numerological reading see Christopher Butler and Alastair Fowler, "Time-Beguiling Sport: Number Symbolism in Shakespeare's *Venus and Adonis*," in *Shakespeare: 1564–1964*, ed. E. A. Bloom (Providence, RI, 1964), 123–35.

traditional epic practice would demand that we should eventually be reminded of such events as Adonis' incestuous parentage and miraculous birth or how Venus, accidentally wounded by Cupid's arrow, became vulnerable to love. Of this background, amply provided by Ovid, the narrator of *Venus and Adonis* shows no awareness whatsoever and it would seem that he relates no more than he has seen or heard as eye-witness or eavesdropper. The story is told in perfectly linear fashion; there will be no flashbacks and (apart from the Mars-Venus episode, 97–114) not much suggestion that either of the protagonists has a relevant past.

The sense of a situation that we have to accept as simply given is reinforced by the opening "Even as" which suggests that three movements which might appear consecutive (the rising sun wakes Adonis who goes to the hunt and is then seen and followed by Venus) are, in fact, simultaneous. There is a sense of convergence as of elements inexorably drawn into collision, and what is significant about this denial of sequence is that (like the absence of flashbacks) it frustrates the urge to explain. In *Venus and Adonis* attraction and repulsion are irreducible facts, to be known only in their manifestations and not in their origins.

The protagonists are, of course, hastening towards paralysis, rushing towards a deadlock that will set in immediately and last for two thirds of the poem in a debate that leads nowhere. Yet to say that is somehow to give a false impression of *Venus and Adonis*. It is not simply that there are so many instances of rapid motion—the horses "outstripping crows" as they race towards the wood (324), the doubling and redoubling of the hare (682), Adonis gliding away from Venus like a shooting star (815), the chariot of Venus herself soaring "through the empty skies" (1191). Even without these memorable images, mobility, in one form or another, would still be essential to our experience of the poem, the source of our initial bewilderment, our growing admiration and our final delight.

One of the most immediately recognizable stylistic peculiarities of *Venus and Adonis* is the two-word transition at the beginning of a stanza: "With this," "By this," "At this," "This said." Such phrases have a disturbingly uncertain status, often turning out to indicate mere sequence rather than the consequence that they seem to promise. Despite the deadlocked situation, we are given the impression of an action so rapid that the narrator, hard-pressed to keep up with events, has to leave the readers to supply their own connections. Characteristically the two-word transition is used to signal the poem's frequent and rapid switches from speech to action ("With this, she seizeth on his sweating palm," 25; "With this he breaketh from her sweet embrace," 811; "This said, she hasteth to a myrtle grove," 865), thus underlining an alternation which is central to the poem's mobility. In Venus, whose conduct creates the narrative rhythm, that alternation takes the extreme form of repeated moves from elaborate rhetorical speeches to bouts of physical violence and back again. The point being made here is not simply that the rhetoric of Venus is ineffective, but that it achieves precisely what rhetoric is intended to avoid. Rhetoric, as the art of persuasion, is traditionally seen as a substitute for violence, it is the weapon of the diplomat not of the soldier: but the rhetoric of Venus, even as it fails to convince Adonis, works the goddess herself up into an erotic frenzy that can only spill over into violence. It is wonderfully appropriate that she should, in the end, imagine a confusion of sexual aggression and persuasion in order to explain the murderous assault on Adonis by the boar

> "Who did not whet his teeth at him again,
> But by a kiss sought to persuade him there."
> (1113–14)

Venus herself is, in many ways, mobility personified. "Variable passions throng her constant woe" (967) says the narrator, describing the combination of fear, despair, revolt and incredulity with which she reacts to the first (inconclusive) evidence that Adonis has been killed.

"Variable passions" is surely an apt way to describe not only the grief of Venus, but her situation from the very beginning of the poem where her first address to Adonis suggests the plurality of desires that she can bring to bear on a single object.

> "Thrice fairer than myself," thus she began,
> "The fields' chief flower, sweet above compare,
> Stain to all nymphs, more lovely than a man,
> More white and red than doves or roses are."
> (7–10)

In this sequence of hyperboles the crucial phrase is "More lovely than a man" which can be read at three levels: (i) more lovely than a mortal, (ii) more lovely than an adult male; (iii) more lovely than the male sex. The love of Venus appears as triply transgressive: transgressive of the cosmic hierarchy by overstepping the bounds between human and divine; transgressive of the generational order because it is the sexual desire of an adult for a child; transgressive of established gender roles because it involves female desire for an essentially feminine beauty. The context draws our immediate attention to the last of these three transgressions. The comparisons with herself and with the nymphs suggest a desire that is, to some extent, both narcissistic and faintly lesbian; and this inward-turning towards her own beauty and her own sex will be consistent with her stubborn refusal to admit the autonomy or otherness of Adonis. Some lines from Philippe Desportes (1546–1606) confirm that the Renaissance Adonis can be seen as appealing to a female taste that is both heterosexual and homosexual:

> Ce mignon si fraizé, qui sert d'homme et de femme,
> A vostre esprit léger, nouvellement surpris:
> Il est vostre Adonis, vous estes sa Cypris.[3]

---

[3] Philippe Desportes, *Diverses Amours et autres oeuvres meslées*, ed. V. E. Graham (Geneva, 1963), 90.

We are probably expected to remember the way Ovid's Venus, addressing Adonis, describes the naked beauty of Atalanta: "Such beauty as is mine or would be yours if you were a woman" (*quale meum, vel quale tuum, si femina fias*, Met, X. 579), but for the modern reader the passage inevitably invites comparison with Shakespeare's own Sonnet 20 on the "Master-Mistress."

> And for a woman wert thou first created,
> Till nature as she wrought thee fell a-doting,
> And by addition me of thee defeated
> By adding one thing to my purpose nothing.
>   But since she pricked thee out for women's pleasure,
>   Mine be thy love and thy love's use their treasure.
>   (9–14)

In the sonnet an apparently transgressive situation, the desire of male for male, is restored to conformity with the natural order by the lover's renunciation of sexual satisfaction. In the narrative poem an apparently natural situation, the desire of female for male, is shown as inwardly transgressive and the lover insists on physical satisfaction. The "one thing" that defeats the speaker of the *Sonnets* would be very much to the purpose of Venus and it turns out to be the one thing she cannot control.

In this context the subsequent couplet becomes richly ironic.

> "Nature that made thee with herself at strife
> Saith that the world hath ending with thy life."
>   (11–12)

Most obviously this means that the world will come to an end if Adonis dies, though there is also the suggestion that the world has signed its own death-warrant in bringing him to life. Since Adonis is mortal, it doesn't really make much difference. Either way, the hyperbole suggests that if nature, by producing Adonis, has succeeded in creating absolute beauty, then she will be left with no justification for her continued existence. Hence the paradox of a nature "with herself at strife," accomplishing her own destruction by producing her only perfect work. But the phrase also suggests the nature which "fell a-doting" of Sonnet 20, a nature too confused in its intentions to function as normative. My point in the first chapter about the way ideologies seek to justify themselves by natural analogies is relevant here. Together with the idea that what is orthodox must be natural comes the assumption that what is natural must be simple—"simply natural" or "naturally simple" as the advertisers put it—and Venus does, indeed, try to persuade Adonis that nature is a straightforward procreative machine. How can this be reconciled with a nature that uses effeminate beauty to excite female desire and that, in the case of Adonis, provides the instrument of procreation without the will to use it? Venus may not be fully aware of her own complex and contradictory urges, but what she will discover in her descent to human love is truly a nature "with herself at strife," too complex, too incoherent and too contradictory to offer any kind of norm. It is this discovery that helps to move the poem from comedy to pathos. Although, at the outset, Venus often seems to belong in Ovid's gallery of brutal and ludicrous Olympian rapists, she gradually draws closer to another Ovidian tradition, that of Byblis, Myrrha, Medea, Dido and Phaedra—the long line of hopelessly transgressive amorous women from whom the poet cannot withhold his sympathy. The problem of a nature that, for all its deceptive promises, frustrates the human urge for simple solutions is what ultimately accounts for the mobility of Venus' discourse—not simply her changing moods or "variable passions," but the inexhaustible profusion and inventivity of her rhetoric, her capacity to change manner and argument without warning. We may sometimes be tempted to see such flexibility as a combination of sheer exuberance and lack of scruple (and Venus surely possesses both these qualities), but in the long run it emerges as the desperate adaptability of someone whose initial certainties have been undermined and who is reduced to clutching at straws.

There is a short step from the mobility of Venus to the shifting perspective of the narrator who seems, at times, to be infected by the goddess's own inconsistency. It is not just that, within the space of two stanzas, he can move from moral condemnation of Venus' sexual aggression ("Forgetting shame's pure blush and honour's wrack," 558) to praise for her persistence ("Things out of hope are compassed oft with vent'ring," 567); even within a single line we can come across extraordinary variations of tone. Take, for example, the celebrated stanza (811–16) where the departing Adonis, compared to a shooting-star, "Leaves love upon her back, deeply distressed" (814). What response is being sought here—aesthetic satisfaction at the aptness of the simile, vindictive laughter at the goddess's physical indignity or sympathy for her distress? It is not helpful to say that we should respond with a combination of all three. *Venus and Adonis* is a disturbing poem because it proceeds through juxtaposition rather than blending, leaving the reader to work out his own eventual amalgamations.

The key to the mobility of the narrator is his apparent lack of hindsight or foresight. He gives no hint as to why he has decided to tell this story or what we are expected to learn from it. His tone is that of someone who has stumbled on the scene by accident. With his eyewitness stance and frequent recourse to the present tense, he gives us what sounds more like a running commentary than a retrospective account. Above all, in his reactions to the verbal and physical performance of Venus, he often functions not as an authoritative guide to the significance of events, but as an audience within the poem, a double of the reader, with the same immediacy of response and the same inevitable improvisations and contradictions. The point will become more clear if we think of love-poetry as normally involving on the one hand a lover (the poet) within the text, and on the other an addressee (the loved one) and an audience (the reader), both outside the text. Such, obviously, is the situation in Shakespeare's *Sonnets*. In *Venus and Adonis*, however (at least up to the departure of Adonis, 811), we have a lover (Venus), an addressee (Adonis) and an audience (the narrator) all within the text. The result is that the rhetoric of Venus, unlike the rhetoric of the sonneteers which it sometimes resembles, is placed in a complex scheme of reception where we can hardly avoid comparing first the reactions of the audience with those of the addressee, and then both these reactions with our own. It follows that *Venus and Adonis*, by encouraging such comparisons, creates unusually self-conscious readers, readers who are constantly being provoked into asking whether their responses are appropriate.

From the very beginning one might say that Venus has trouble striking the right tone. The opening courtesies ("Vouchsafe, thou wonder," "Deign this favour," 13–15) would be conventional enough as the *captatio benevolentiae* of a male seducer, but sound rather groveling coming from a woman and a goddess. The promises that they introduce are a curious mixture of hidden knowledge ("A thousand honey secrets," 16) and prelapsarian innocence ("where never serpent hisses," 17). The invitation "Here come and sit" (17) may indicate either the ground or, more probably, Venus' lap where, for his "meed" (with a pun on "mead"), Adonis will discover the vaginal honeypot beloved of pornographers. The honey is, however, not merely erotic; it also suggests the maternal tempting of a child with sweetmeats, and Shakespeare may intend us to hear the mother-rhyme in "I'll smother thee with kisses" (18). The verb, with its blend of physical aggression and over-protectiveness, is typical of Venus and should lead one to appreciate why Adonis later argues (523–28) that intercourse with her would be a threat to his development rather than a step towards manhood.

Venus, in any case, seems to recognize the negative implications of her own imagery and seeks to correct them. Just as earlier she had promised secret knowledge without loss of innocence, so now she promises satisfaction without loss of desire.

> "And yet not cloy thy lips with loathed satiety,
> But rather famish them amid their plenty."
> (19–20)

The lines recall *inopem me copia fecit* ("My riches beggar me," *Met.* III. 466), a paradox that works negatively for Ovid's Narcissus and for the unprocreative youth of Shakespeare's Sonnet 1 ("Making a famine where abundance lies"), but positively for Cleopatra who is celebrated by Enobarbus precisely because "she makes hungry / Where most she satisfies" (*Antony*, II. ii. 243–44). Here, like so many of Venus' inducements, it cuts both ways at once, for she cannot promise endless pleasure without simultaneously presenting the sexual appetite as one that cannot be assuaged. There is a similar double-edged promise in the ambiguity of "wasted":

> "A summer's day will seem an hour but short,
> Being wasted in such time-beguiling sport."
> (23–24)

"Waste" may be just a synonym for "spend," but one can hardly forget that Adonis, on his way to the hunt, is not at a loose end and that Venus' attempt at seduction will turn out to be a waste of time for both of them. Moreover, Venus' own eagerness belies her suggestion that lovemaking is merely an agreeable way of passing the time. More apparently seductive is the rhetorical virtuosity of "Ten kisses short as one, one long as twenty" (22). Instead of the predictable antimetabole ABBA which might suggest a vicious circle, we are given ABBA+, conveying the sense of an upward spiral which, rather than returning to the starting-point, rises to an ever-higher intensity where the confusion of time (what's long? what's short?) eliminates the problem of alternating states. But time, after all, will not be beguiled and the poem will continue to remind us of its passing (177–80, 529–34, 727–32, 853–58).

The alternance of speech and physical action that dictates the narrative rhythm of the poem also creates much of its comedy. A rhetoric that seems to have all the time in the world and that neglects no opportunity for elegant *copia* is regularly interrupted by action that is precipitate, bungled and grotesquely gymnastic. We are constantly reminded of the disjunction between the verbal and physical expressions of desire. Coleridge famously remarked of *Venus and Adonis* that "you seem to be told nothing, but to see and hear everything,"[4] but seeing and hearing are different in their effects and the experience of the voyeur may clash with that of the eavesdropper. At this stage, however, what we witness seems to be a relatively mild form of physical initiative.

> With this, she seizeth on his sweating palm,
> The precedent of pith and livelihood,
> And, trembling in her passion, calls it balm,
> Earth's sovereign salve to do a goddess good.
> (25–28)

Like Astrophil in a similar situation, Venus uses her hands to make "tongue's language plain" (*Astrophil and Stella*, Eighth Song). She also hopes that the hand of Adonis will say what his tongue does not. Having promised her own "honey secrets," she seeks evidence of a responsive sexual lubrification in his "sweating palm." Gypsies try to read palms in a sense favorable to their clients: since Venus here is both gypsy and client, she has no difficulty in making the hand provide the answer she wants. Her misreading predictably leads to more hyperbole which culminates in more physical action. As if ashamed of her own earthiness, she renames the sweat with imagery that combines the politico-religious (the anointing of a monarch) with the medical. By a startling inversion of the cosmic hierarchy it is the earthly subject who produces a salve to heal the queen and goddess.

---

[4] *Biographia Literaria*, ii. 15.

Holding hands with someone on horseback is not exactly easy. Venus profits from the situation to pull Adonis down to her own level, and her strength derives not from any supernatural power but from the surge of energy that follows this first physical contact:

> Being so enraged, desire doth lend her force,
> Courageously to pluck him from his horse.
> (29–30)

It seems to augur well for the goddess's attempt to pluck the flower or fruit of the youth's virginity (127–32). The equestrian metaphor was frequently used to illustrate the way reason should govern the passions and, in this light, Adonis' failure to remain in the saddle might herald a surrender to the senses. This "precedent" turns out to be no less deceptive than the sweating palm. Venus, one assumes, sees the event as a first step towards taking the horse's place underneath Adonis; but it is when she finally achieves the desired position and gets Adonis to mount her (595–600) that she will be most clearly frustrated.

The equestrian metaphor is, indeed, deeply ambivalent since it can suggest not only the dominance of reason over the passions but also a powerful sexual energy (Cleopatra's "O happy horse, to bear the weight of Antony!," *Antony*, I. v. 21). In the latter case the easy dismounting of Adonis would no longer look so promising. The dilemma of Venus who cannot resist using on Adonis the strength that she wishes he would use on her is neatly embodied in a hilarious cartoon-like vignette:

> Over one arm, the lusty courser's rein;
> Under her other was the tender boy.
> (31–32)

With one arm she holds the lustiness of the horse and with the other the tenderness of Adonis. What she wants but cannot have is the lustiness and the tenderness united in the same object. She appears momentarily as a gigantic walking antithesis.

One aspect of the poem's mobility is the way its symbolism refuses to respect any fixed pattern. In the conventional scheme of color connotations we would expect the passion of Venus and the chastity of Adonis to be associated with red and white respectively. Here, though Venus is fire and Adonis is frost, red becomes the color of both protagonists.

> She red and hot as coals of glowing fire,
> He red for shame, but frosty in desire.
> (35–36)

The poem's pervasive red-white imagery, though it provides a unifying thread, does not offer a convenient key to interpretation: on the contrary, it makes our reactions progressively more interrogative, reminding us that we are on shifting ground. Here red wars with red; later white will war with white (361–66); on other occasions the struggle between red and white will take place within each of the protagonists. In this case, the unexpected opposition of red to red is more than a typical piece of late Petrarchist ingenuity. The Adonis who pouts "in a dull disdain" and who is "unapt to toy" (33–34) might appear as merely negative, as the simple antithesis of passion; but his redness, his blushing for shame, reminds us that chastity, no less than desire, can be a passionate commitment—as it is for Isabella in *Measure for Measure*.[5] The impression is confirmed when, a few stanzas later (49–52), the context gives an unexpected turn to the conventional antitheses of burning and quenching, dryness and moisture. In the Petrarchan tradition it would be a male lover who burns with a fire that neither his own tears nor the cold chastity of his mistress can quench. Here it is a female lover who seeks with her tears to quench the fiery chastity ("maiden burning") of the reluctant male.

---

[5] Characters who defend their chastity get rather a rough deal in contemporary criticism. It might help if we started to describe them as "victims of sexual harassment."

Once again chastity is allowed a degree of emotional intensity. If it were not so, if Adonis did not have some passion of his own, he would be far less interesting as an antagonist of Venus.

The youth and the goddess now find themselves literally on the same level, but the result is not to be an Edenic communication between mortal and immortal. Having tethered the horse with a dexterity that goes some way towards countering our impression of her bulkiness, Venus now attempts "to tie the rider."

> Backward she pushed him, as she would be thrust,
> And governed him in strength, though not in lust.
> (41–42)

The syntactic structure associates pushing with strength and thrusting with lust, thus preventing us from seeing the two verbs as synonyms. Venus has the strength to push, but thrusting, with its penetrative connotations, is precisely what she cannot, and Adonis will not do. Her strength becomes a weakness, putting her (again quite literally) in a false position. And yet the scene seems all set for the kind of pastoral idyll that Renaissance poetry provides with such profusion. The reader could be expected to remember what Ovid makes of the situation.

> 'et, ecce,
> opportuna sua blanditur populus umbra,
> datque torum caespes: libet hac requiescere tecum'
> (et requievit) 'humo' pressitque et gramen et ipsum
> inque sinu iuvenis posita cervice reclinis
> sic ait ac mediis interserit oscula verbis.
> (*Met*, X. 554–59)

'And see, a poplar, happily at hand, invites us with its shade, and here is grassy turf for couch. I would fain rest here on the grass with you'. So saying, she reclined upon the ground and on him, and, pillowing her head against his breast and mingling kisses with her words, she told the following tale.

Shakespeare uses the same details to produce a very different effect:

> So soon was she along as he was down,
> Each leaning on their elbows and their hips.
> Now doth she stroke his cheek, now doth he frown,
> And 'gins to chide, but soon she stops his lips,
>   And, kissing, speaks, with lustful language broken:
>   "If thou wilt chide, thy lips shall never open."
> (43–48)

Ovid's poplar has already been replaced in the previous stanza by "a ragged bough" (37) which, to judge by later events, gives no shade whatsoever. Elbows and hips do not figure largely in Renaissance blazons of the human body and they convey a sense of awkwardness and discomfort that will be familiar to anyone who has tried to make love in the open air without an inflatable mattress. Where, in Ovid, we have Venus "mingling kisses with her words," Shakespeare gives us "And, kissing, speaks, with lustful language broken" so that, instead of a pleasant blend, we get a sense of dysfunction and disjunction, a failure to harmonize speech and gesture. A standard topos of pastoral poetry has been treated in a fashion that verges on iconoclasm.

Adonis begins to speak, but the reader is not allowed to hear his voice which is stifled for a second time by the kiss of Venus.

> He saith she is immodest, blames her miss;
> What follows more she murders with a kiss.
> (53–54)

As I shall argue later, too much has been made of the association between this murderous kiss and the destructive embrace of the boar (1109–18), especially by those who insist on downgrading characterization in the hope of finding some tidy moral or allegorical message. At this stage, it should be enough to affirm that, although the poem recognizes a potentially destructive element in sexual desire, it does not necessarily equate desire with destructiveness. Thus, in the following stanza, we need to remember that the limits of a simile are part of its meaning.

> Even as an empty eagle, sharp by fast,
> Tires with her beak on feathers, flesh, and bone,
> Shaking her wings, devouring all in haste
> Till either gorge be stuffed or prey be gone,
>   Even so she kissed his brow, his cheek, his chin,
>   And where she ends she doth anew begin.
>   (55–60)

This is undeniably unpleasant and recalls Ovid's Olympian rapists in their most bestial forms. But Venus, unlike Jupiter, does not actually assume the shape of an eagle any more than she will later transform herself into a boar. And the couplet reminds us that, for all its violence, this is still kissing not cannibalism. The simile tells us not so much what the desire of Venus is really like as what it looks like to the observer and, no doubt, feels like to Adonis. We immediately discover how it feels to Venus herself.

> Forced to content, but never to obey,
> Panting he lies and breatheth in her face.
> She feedeth on the steam as on a prey
> And calls it heavenly moisture, air of grace,
>   Wishing her cheeks were gardens full of flowers,
>   So they were dewed with such distilling showers.
>   (61–66)

Here we have a characteristic aspect of the poem's mobility. The contrast with the previous stanza could hardly be greater and yet we recognize that we are being offered different perspectives on the same reality. "Feedeth" and "prey" continue the predatory imagery, but what looked to the narrator like the satisfaction of sheer physical hunger is transformed by Venus' renaming into something like a spiritual experience ("heavenly moisture," "air of grace"), paradoxically granted by a mortal to a goddess.[6] Where Venus had seemed to embody the law of the jungle, she is now rephrased as a cultivated garden in need of refreshing rain. That the renaming involves self-delusion does not constitute the "empty eagle" as objective reality. Body language is no more reliable than verbal language. The physical and verbal manifestations of desire are equally revealing and misleading and, perhaps, one may serve to correct the other. The narrator, indeed, after juxtaposing the event as it appears and the event as it is subjectively reconstructed, invites us to adopt a more balanced view.

> Look how a bird lies tangled in a net,
> So fastened in her arms Adonis lies.
> (67–68)

Adonis is still a prey of sorts, but the birdcatching simile would suggest that he is in more danger of being tamed and kept for amusement than of being eaten alive (anticipating "Like a wild bird being tamed with too much handling," 560). The real issue is not that Venus threatens to destroy Adonis, but that she tries to deprive him of his freedom. And lest anyone should argue that this amounts to the same thing, it should be remembered that it is Adonis' regained liberty rather than his temporary captivity that brings about his death. The kissing only looks like murder and a metaphorical eagle is not so dangerous as an unmetaphorical boar.

Adonis responds with an anger that adds to his beauty and thus increases the desire of Venus just as her desire increases his anger; and this vicious circle inspires a couplet which, in the immediate context, points to Venus (the "rank" current of her lust), but which can also be seen as a generalization that is relevant to both protagonists:

---

[6] See Dubrow, 29. "Venus' predilection for renaming the world typically assumes one form in particular: she tries to transform the material into the spiritual."

> Rain added to a river that is rank
> Perforce will force it overflow the bank.
> (71–72)

Venus and Adonis are condemned to provoke each other to excess and the goddess's first assault ends by setting up a process of reciprocal exasperation.

The overflowing already suggests the first of Venus' many minor orgasms. Her energy is momentarily exhausted and she returns to verbal persuasion:

> Still she entreats and prettily entreats,
> For to a pretty ear she tunes her tale.
> Still is he sullen, still he lours and frets
> 'Twixt crimson shame and anger ashy-pale.
> > Being red, she loves him best; and being white,
> > Her best is bettered with a more delight.
> > (77–78)

The narrator's rhetoric, with its anaphora, epistrophe, polyptoton and, of course, its red-white antithesis, enacts the prettiness of which it speaks. In a poem that revels in the observation of small things (the caterpillar, the divedapper, the snail), the "pretty ear" of Adonis need not be taken as a straightforward synecdoche. The detail suggests the delicate, finely-chiseled beauty of Adonis, and Venus' admiration for her beloved's ear—not normally an object of intense erotic attraction—has a tender, intimate quality like maternal absorption in the anatomical minutiae of a newborn son.

In this cooler climate Venus appeals for "one sweet kiss" with a blend of military and commercial imagery ("take truce," "countless debt") which reflects her own hesitation between force and negotiation (79–84). Her "contending tears" prolong the watery atmosphere of the rainfed river (71–72) and provide an appropriate setting for the divedapper.

> Upon this promise did he raise his chin,
> Like a divedapper peering through a wave
> Who, being looked on, ducks as quickly in—
> So offers he to give what she did crave.
> (85–88)

The simile has been celebrated as evidence of Shakespeare's precise natural observation, an image "so vivid as to snatch your attention from the story,"[7] but it is surely the aptness that makes it so memorable. Not only does it convey the rapid, tentative, half-curious and half-fearful movement of Adonis, but the very name combines the sense of evasiveness ("dive") with the neat ("dapper") and somewhat miniature quality of his beauty, so different from the protean expansiveness of Venus. It has been argued that Adonis, in seeming to offer and then refusing the kiss, is revealed as a male coquette who enjoys arousing desire that he does not intend to satisfy.[8] The poem, however, leaves little doubt that Adonis is genuinely offended by Venus' unsought attentions and there is nothing to suggest that he enjoys teasing her. It is more likely that the narrator has, for a moment, assumed the perspective of Venus who, as we know, is adept at misreading the signs.

The plight of Venus continues to be imaged in the aquatic atmosphere created by her "contending tears":

> Never did passenger in summer's heat
> More thirst for drink than she for this good turn.
> Her help she sees, but help she cannot get.
> She bathes in water, yet her fire must burn.
> (91–94)

---

[7] George Wyndham, ed., *The Poems of Shakespeare* (London, 1898), xxxiv.

[8] J. D. Jahn, "The Lamb of Lust: the Role of Adonis in Shakespeare's *Venus and Adonis*," *Shakespeare Studies* 6 (1970), 11–25.

The familiar Petrarchan paradox of the lover who unites water and fire is reinforced by the implicit allusion (explicit at 599) to Tantalus. In this highly literary context, the colloquial "this good turn" draws attention to itself as functioning on several levels: as the literal turn of Adonis' lips towards her, as the good turn which is the second corporal work of mercy (to give drink to the thirsty), and, perhaps, as "the best turn i'th'bed" (*Antony*, II. v. 59). There is a subtle conflation of immediate need and ultimate objective.

> "O pity," gan she cry, "flint-hearted boy!
> 'Tis but a kiss I beg—why art thou coy?"
> (95–96)

Even Venus, with her talent for self-deception, can hardly believe that a kiss is all she wants. To start with such a minimal request is a humiliating strategy for a goddess to adopt, and for Venus, in any case, self-abasement and self-advertisement are only two sides of the same coin which is self-concern. She now seeks to enhance her own attractions by giving a wisely expurgated version of the Homeric tale of her affair with Mars (97–114), omitting the net which the jealous Vulcan throws over the lovers and their embarrassing exposure to the voyeuristic gaze of the assembled gods. Shakespeare may be offering some tempting bait to moralists and allegorists. Moralists, in the tradition of *Ovide moralisé*, would see in the Mars-Venus story a warning that hidden adulteries always come to light and a monitory example of how the hero can be distracted from the active life by the blandishments of sensual pleasure. Elizabethan readers might well have remembered Spenser's Bower of Bliss with Verdaunt lying besotted in the arms of Acrasia (*FQ*, II. xii) or Tasso's Rinaldo neglecting the liberation of Jerusalem in the embrace of Armida (*Gerusalemme Liberata*, XVI). The supine position of Mars and his abandoned arms, so often represented in Renaissance paintings, would in this context indicate a fall from grace reminiscent of Samson's infatuation with Delilah or Adam's culpable subjection to Eve. Adonis, by implication, would become a rather unlikely Christian hero who succeeds where Adam and Samson, Verdaunt and Rinaldo, have all failed.

Allegorists might take a different line. Even in antiquity there were attempts to purge the tale of its scandalous and titillating aspects. Neoplatonists, taking their cue perhaps from Lucretius (*De Rerum Natura*, I. 29–43), saw the conjunction of Mars and Venus as the perfect union of the irascible and concupiscible, of male and female qualities, giving birth to Harmony. The suspended weapons would now be emblematic not of abandoned heroism but of universal peace and cosmic order.[9]

The tradition, therefore, is ambivalent and, though Shakespeare may be teasing his readers with hints of a possible allegory, neither the homilies of *Ovide moralisé* nor the visionary solemnities of the Neoplatonists will provide a convincing explanation of how this episode works in *Venus and Adonis*. If we look at the story as Shakespeare found it in the *Metamorphoses* (IV. 171–89), we find that the tone is one of libertine flippancy. When Vulcan drops his net over the naked adulterers and displays their shame to the summoned Olympians, Ovid (like Homer before him) makes it clear that the spectators are less outraged than stimulated and amused:

> illi iacuere ligati
> turpiter, atque aliquis de dis non tristibus optat
> sic fieri turpis; superi risere, diuque
> haec fuit in toto notissima fabula caelo.
> (*Met*, IV. 186–89)

There lay the two in chains, disgracefully, and some one of the merry gods prayed that he too might be so disgraced. The gods laughed, and for a long time this story was the talk of heaven.

---

[9] For positive readings of the Mars-Venus story see Edgar Wind, *Pagan Mysteries of the Renaissance* (rev. ed., London, 1980), 82–94.

Venus tells her expurgated version in something of the same spirit, assuming that Adonis will find it more enticing than immoral. What we need to examine, therefore, is how far this ecphrasis really serves her purposes. On a first reading, it would seem hard to envisage the dainty, pretty-eared Adonis as a successor to "the stern and direful god of war" with his "sinewy neck" (98–99). A potential lover is rarely encouraged by praise of his predecessor and if Mars embodies the kind of virility needed to satisfy Venus, then Adonis might well shrink from the task. But Venus is catholic in her tastes and she may, after all, be making a useful psychological move. Adonis' preference for hunting suggests a young man anxious to prove himself in what is traditionally a substitute for war as an initiation into adult manhood. It would make sense for Venus to remind him that the sexual arena also offers affirmations worthy of the aspiring male. Why should Adonis refuse a conquest worthy of Mars himself?

Unfortunately, this is not quite the argument that Venus makes and her attempt to equate love and war as analogous fields of masculine prowess remains riddled with contradictions. Instead of urging Adonis to imitate the conquest of Mars, she concludes with the punchline:

> "O, be not proud, nor brag not of thy might,
> For mast'ring her that foiled the god of fight."
> (113–14)

Venus is betrayed by her own vanity, by her need for self-advertisement and reassurance. Rather than showing the episode as a victory on the part of Mars that Adonis would do well to emulate, she presents it as her own conquest in terms that can only confirm any fears that Adonis may have about sexual intercourse as a loss of his male autonomy.

> "Over my altars hath he hung his lance,
> His battered shield, his uncontrollèd crest,
> And for my sake hath learned to sport and dance,
> To toy, to wanton, dally, smile, and jest,

> Scorning his churlish drum and ensign red,
> Making my arms his field, his tent my bed.
>
> "Thus he that over-ruled I overswayed,
> Leading him prisoner in a red-rose chain.
> Strong-tempered steel his stronger strength obeyed,
> Yet was he servile to my coy disdain."
> (103–12)

The elegant chiasmus of "Making my arms his field, his tent my bed" may establish the analogy between love and war, but Venus leaves us in no doubt that in this struggle it is the woman who emerges as the victor. She had done well to avoid any reference to Vulcan's net, but her own "red-rose chain" might seem to Adonis only a prettified version of a hardly less disgraceful humiliation. There is not much left of the military dignity of Mars after an extraordinary list of synonyms (sport, toy, wanton, dally, jest) has reduced him to the Malvolio role of fatuous lover. The "lance" and "uncontrollèd crest" lose their phallic power by being, as it were, detached from their owner and displayed as trophies on the altar of Venus. This is not so much a virile conquest as virility's defeat. The logic of Venus' argument is superficially sound: if I have conquered Mars and you conquer me, then you must be a greater conqueror than Mars. But it is a logic that fails to take account of gender roles and male solidarity. For all Venus' talk of "mast'ring her that foiled the god of fight," the emphasis falls on the emasculating power of female sexuality and is likely to serve Adonis more as a warning than as an inducement.

By recounting her affair with Mars, Venus attempts to present herself as an irresistibly seductive woman while still discreetly reminding Adonis of her Olympian status. We might have expected her to make a good deal more of her divinity. If Shakespeare does not allow her to do so, this may be because he wants her to maintain our sympathy and thus prefers to stress the thoroughness of her descent to the human level. We may also suppose that Venus herself is intelligent enough to understand that frequent appeal to her divine powers and prerogatives is likely to be counter-productive. Here, as if some second sense made her aware of Adonis' unspoken objections to her rhetoric of conquest ("over-ruled," "overswayed," "mast'ring," "servile," "prisoner," 109–14), she rapidly changes direction and insists on love as mutual exchange between equal partners:

> "Touch but my lips with those fair lips of thine—
> Though mine be not so fair, yet are they red—
> The kiss shall be thine own as well as mine.
> What seest thou in the ground? Hold up thy head,
>   Look in mine eyeballs: there thy beauty lies.
>   Then why not lips on lips, since eyes in eyes?"
> (115–20)

Beauty is on both sides—the kiss that is given and taken becomes common property; Adonis will find reflected in the eyes of Venus the image of himself. The latter conceit is a conventional way of indicating mutuality in love ("My face in thine eye, thine in mine appears" as Donne puts it in "The Good-Morrow"), but the use that Venus makes of it suggests that she is trying to calm any fears aroused in the Mars-Venus stanzas that lovemaking involves some loss of the self. She argues, in fact, that love will provide a stronger self-image, cleverly combining a plea for reciprocity with an appeal to the narcissism that she suspects in Adonis (a suspicion made explicit at 157–62). The self-image that Adonis seeks will be discovered not "in the ground" but in the regard of the Other. Beauty resides quite literally in the eye of the beholder.

From the potentially treacherous terrain of Adonis' selfhood Venus moves to apparently safer ground with persuasions appropriate for convincing a bashful but not entirely unwilling virgin. If Adonis is ashamed to make love in broad daylight, they can create night by closing their eyes; if he is afraid of scandal, he can be sure that the flowers will tell no tales; if, as Venus might fear, he remembers the exposure of Mars and Venus in Vulcan's net, he is promised that "our sport is not in sight" (124). Her basic argument is, predictably, the Catullan *carpe diem*:

> "The tender spring upon thy tempting lip
> Shows thee unripe; yet mayst thou still be tasted.
> Make use of time, let not advantage slip.
> Beauty within itself should not be wasted.
>   Fair flowers that are not gathered in their prime
>   Rot, and consume themselves in little time."
>   (127-32)

Yet even here Venus fails to reassure. The taste metaphor occurs before we have forgotten the devouring fury of Venus as "the empty eagle" (55-60); the association of temptation and fruit has an inappropriate biblical resonance and comes awkwardly in an argument that consumption preserves beauty from corruption. The crux is "prime" which can be glossed either as the springtime of life or as the period of its full fruition or maturity. If we take "prime" as maturity, then, as Adonis will argue later (415-20), unripeness becomes a valid justification for sexual abstinence. There is no need to convict Venus of dishonesty: she may genuinely want to believe that Adonis is ripe for love, but she cannot help hinting that his unripeness is what makes him attractive. The ambiguity of "prime" reflects the confusion of her own sentiments.

The emphasis on the youthfulness of Adonis, combined with the reminiscence of her own experience in the Mars-Venus stanzas, threatens to open an age-gap between the protagonists. Once again Venus has the sharpness and flexibility to head off unspoken objections by reminding Adonis that her charms are anything but overblown. This she does by exorcising the specter of old age with a massive asyndeton of fifteen epithets describing everything that she is not and culminating in the splendidly vigorous "lacking juice" which recalls all the imagery of tasting and sexual lubrification:

> "Were I hard-favoured, foul, or wrinkled-old,
> Ill-nurtured, crooked, churlish, harsh in voice,
> O'er-worn, despisèd, rheumatic, and cold,
> Thick-sighted, barren, lean, and lacking juice,
>   Then mightst thou pause, for then I were not for thee.
>   But having no defects, why dost abhor me?"
>   (133–38)

This is followed by a corresponding list of positive qualities calculated to attain two objectives: first, to remind Adonis that age is irrelevant to a goddess who is endowed with eternal youth ("My beauty as the spring doth yearly grow," 141) and second, to counteract the sense of physical weight with images of lightness. Whereas previously her desire had been associated with descent and with the element of earth (Adonis pulled down from his horse, the lovers falling to the ground, Adonis as an imprisoned bird), now it is related to the element of fire whose natural motion is to rise:

> "Love is a spirit all compact of fire,
> Not gross to sink, but light, and will aspire."
>   (149–50)

It is, perhaps, because Venus is aware of the depths of her descent that she needs to see herself as embodying this lightness—"with long, dishevelled hair," tripping on the green, dancing on the sands and leaving no footprint (146–48)—more like a figure from Botticelli's *Primavera* than the muscular matron we have seen so far. And yet, as so often, she comes near to being undone by her own hyperbole:

> "Witness this primrose bank whereon I lie:
> These forceless flowers like sturdy trees support me.
> Two strengthless doves will draw me through the sky
> From morn till night, even where I list to sport me.
>   Is love so light, sweet boy, and may it be
>   That thou should think it heavy unto thee?"
>   (151–56)

The effect of the first two lines is not to make Venus light but to make the primroses enormous in order to support her bulk. The "strengthless doves" are more effective in context and contribute to the irony of the poem's conclusion where they intervene not to carry the goddess off on an endless round of presumably amorous "sport," but to lift her out of a world where her descent to love has ended in defeat. As for the punning on the physical and psychological senses of "light" and "heavy," it is, in the circumstances, distinctly tactless since it risks reminding Adonis of the disjunction between the verbal and physical manifestations of desire. As he hears Venus speak of her own and love's lightness, he is actually being pinned to the ground: the goddess is impressive in more ways than one.

Having established to her own satisfaction that her seductiveness is beyond question, Venus has no choice but to seek the cause of her frustration in some defect of Adonis whom she promptly accuses of narcissism. It is, in its way, a form of compliment since it assumes that the only beauty which could prevent Adonis from admiring her must be his own:

> "Is thine own heart to thine own face affected?
> Can thy right hand seize love upon thy left?
> Then woo thyself, be of thyself rejected;
> Steal thine own freedom, and complain on theft.
>   Narcissus so himself himself forsook,
>   And died to kiss his shadow in the brook."
> (157–62)

This, one might think, is a bit rich coming from a woman who has spent the last three stanzas cataloguing her own attractions—especially when the poem offers no evidence that Adonis is even conscious of his own beauty. If, however, we take Narcissus as an example of what it means to be obsessed with selfhood, then the accusation does carry some weight. Ovid seems to have seen the Narcissus story in this light when he makes Tiresias prophesy that Narcissus will live a long life "if he ne'er know himself" (*si se non noverit*, *Met*, III. 346–48). The irony of the tale is that Tiresias turns out to be subtly wrong. It is obsession with the self rather than true self-knowledge that destroys Narcissus, for the image that he contemplates in the pool is not a knowable reality: "He loves an unsubstantial hope and thinks that substance which is only shadow" (*spem sine corpore amat, corpus putat esse, quod umbra est, Met*, III. 417). Shakespeare gives Adonis the same concern for self-knowledge ("Before I know myself, seek not to know me," 525) and he lends Venus the rhetorical figures of antithesis, chiasmus, epizeuxis, and ploke (the stanza's fourfold repetition of "self") to convey the paradox that to seek the self is to lose it.

Venus' argument is impressively marshaled and it has been readily used by readers who wish to make Adonis responsible for his own destruction. And yet, in context, it is weakened (not invalidated) by the motives and character of the speaker. We are invited to conclude that true self-knowledge is only to be gained through knowledge of others, but Venus shows little sign of wanting to know Adonis in anything but the carnal sense, and almost everything about her desire indicates less an outgoing towards Adonis than an attempt to absorb him. There is more than one form of narcissism.

From the somewhat bantering tone of her attack on narcissism Venus now shifts to a graver register as she presents the issue in essentially moral terms ("Things growing to themselves are growth's abuse," "Thou wast begot; to get it is thy duty," 166–68). It is difficult at first to take her seriously. We suspect that she resorts to moralizing only because her physical charms have proved insufficiently persuasive. Unlike the speaker of the matrimonial sonnets (1–17) who uses much the same arguments, she has a vested interest which is betrayed by analogies that suggest her own need for immediate satisfaction rather than any moral imperative.

> "Torches are made to light, jewels to wear,
> Dainties to taste, fresh beauty for the use,
> Herbs for their smell, and sappy plants to bear."
>   (163–65)

The fertility of "sappy plants" cannot quite correct the impression that Adonis is simply being constituted as one more object of conspicuous consumption. The phrase "By law of nature thou art bound to breed" (171) hovers rather cynically between enjoining procreation as a duty and presenting it as a biological impulse that leaves him with no choice. For all Venus' insistence on breeding as a means of self-perpetuation ("And so in spite of death thou dost survive," 173), Adonis may well feel that to be seen as a cog in a vast procreative machine does little to enhance his dignity.

We need not, however, see the arguments of Venus as entirely disingenuous. We remember that, in her very first speech, desire for Adonis had been associated with fear of his death ("the world hath ending with thy life," 12). It is fear as much as lust that will eventually fuel her rhetoric and give a desperate and pathetic edge to the incongruity of her moralizing. That fear will loom ever larger until it becomes finally focused on the figure of the boar.

As if to banish any dark thoughts engendered by Venus' talk of death and survival, the narrator—in a switch typical of the poem—reminds us of the physical indignity of her position:

> By this, the lovesick queen began to sweat,
> For where they lay the shadow had forsook them,
> And Titan, tired in the midday heat,
> With burning eye did hotly overlook them,
>   Wishing Adonis had his team to guide,
>   So he were like him, and by Venus' side.
>   (175–80)

The sign that had proved misleading when Venus read the "sweating palm" of Adonis (25–26) is unequivocal in her own case and we are not tempted to see it simply as a consequence of "the midday heat." The heating is, indeed, reciprocal. Titan's beams warm the already overheated goddess and he, in turn, is warmed by the erotic spectacle that he contemplates. The couplet reminds us of the god who, in Homer and Ovid, wished to take the place of Mars under Vulcan's net. Venus was, perhaps, being over-optimistic when she promised "our sport is not in sight" (124). Titan, as voyeur, recalls the eyewitness situation of the narrator and also evokes the reaction that Shakespeare could have expected from his male readers—especially "the younger sort" who might envy Adonis the opportunity of being initiated into the mysteries of sex by an experienced older woman. Such readers, already made spectators of an erotic performance, are now offered the added refinement of watching someone watching.

Adonis has already attempted to rebut the arguments of Venus ("He saith she is immodest, blames her miss," 53), but now, for the first time, we are allowed to hear his voice: "Fie, no more of love! / The sun doth burn my face; I must remove" (185–86). At least one critic has argued that Adonis is afraid of having his lovely complexion ruined by sunburn,[10] but the context of "lazy sprite," "disliking eye," and "louring brows" (181–83) suggests the sulky teenager rather than the narcissist or the coquette. The real point about this petulant remark is that its irrelevance misleads us (and Venus) into thinking that Adonis has nothing to say for himself. It will come as all the more of a surprise when, in his last long speech (769–810), he finally puts his case with such devastating effect. At this stage, his "bare excuses" (188) serve only to provide Venus with a new springboard for her rhetorical somersaults. If Adonis is too hot, her sighs will produce a "gentle wind" and her hair a shadow; if her hair also burns, she will quench the burning with her tears (189–92). Venus is, after all, more in danger of incineration than Adonis since, lying "between that sun and thee" (194), she is being grilled on both sides:

---

[10] Jahn, 12.

> "And were I not immortal, life were done
> Between this heavenly and earthly sun."
> (197–98)

We are not allowed to forget that Venus is immobilizing Adonis by lying on top of him. That she should, at the same time, remind us of her divine status and indulge in a Neoplatonist renaming of Adonis only increases our sense of the grotesque.

Venus is too professional a rhetorician to neglect the inevitable homophone pun on "sun/son" which leads into a familiar seduction ploy:

> "Art thou a woman's son, and canst not feel
> What 'tis to love, how want of love tormenteth?
> O, had thy mother borne so hard a mind,
> She had not brought forth thee, but died unkind."
> (201–04)

Jonathan Bate believes that Venus is (rather tactlessly) alluding to the mother of Adonis, the hapless Myrrha who gave birth to Adonis as the result of her incestuous love for her father, Cinyras. This would certainly give added density to the ambiguities of "unkind." It would have been better for Myrrha to have been "unkind" by withholding her sexual favors rather than to have indulged a passion for her own kin that was "unkind" in the sense of unnatural. The importance we attach to the Myrrha story must depend on the rather moot question of how much Ovid Shakespeare expected or wanted his readers to remember. That some readers certainly were reminded of the scabrous Ovidian context is proved by such prurient offshoots of *Venus and Adonis* as William Barksted's *Mirrha, the Mother of Adonis; or Lustes Prodegies* (1607), Henry Austin's *The Scourge of Venus* (1613) and James Gresham's *The Picture of Incest* (1626). Yet if Shakespeare ever does recall Myrrha, he does so in a very marginal and oblique fashion. Here, for instance, the allusion to "thy mother" grows so naturally out of "Art thou a woman's son" that one is not invited to stop and inquire who that mother might have been. The passage is, in any case, already rich with less sinister ironies. It seems counter-productive for Venus to evoke motherhood when she already runs a serious risk of appearing old enough to be Adonis' mother herself. What is more, the appeal to motherhood is traditionally a strategy for seducing female virgins. Venus fails to make the necessary adaptation "O, had thy *father* borne so hard a mind" and thus allows her argument to become entangled once again in the awkward inversion of gender roles.

The rhetoric of Venus is both precipitous and elaborate, breathless and long-winded, less like a marathon than a series of extended sprints. No sooner has one argument been brought to something that looks like a conclusion than she is off with bewildering speed on a new tack. As if unaware of the inconsistency, she now follows up her insistence on procreation with a renewed plea for "one poor kiss" (207)—only to throw away any tactical advantage that this reduced demand might have gained by promising (or threatening) that one kiss will turn into three:

> "Give me one kiss, I'll give it thee again,
> And one for int'rest, if thou wilt have twain."
> (209–10)

Venus' argumentation hovers between the unscrupulous and the naive, but she has little confidence in its success ("Speak, fair, but speak fair words, or else be mute," 208). One begins to wonder whether her inexhaustible eloquence is really designed to persuade or whether it does not become, more effectively, a means of prolonging the status quo, the verbal equivalent of the physical oppression by which she postpones the departure of Adonis. The very mobility of her rhetoric suggests that the intrinsic power of the argument matters less than the fact that it keeps the discourse going.

Venus reserves language for herself; the only response she will allow in Adonis is strictly non-verbal. Lacking such a response, she challenges his virility:

> "Fie, lifeless picture, cold and senseless stone,
> Well painted idol, image dull and dead,
> Statue contenting but the eye alone,
> Thing like a man, but of no woman bred."
> (211–14)

The conventional sculpture analogy gains a new relevance if we remember the story of Pygmalion (*Met*, X. 243–97) which, in Ovid, immediately precedes that of Adonis' parents, Cinyras and Myrrha. Venus had answered the prayer of Pygmalion and transformed the "senseless stone" of his carving into a living woman; but she cannot perform an analogous miracle in her own interest. And, since she is herself the goddess of love, there is no divinity to whom she can pray. The stony quality of Adonis is ironically appropriate in that he happens to be the direct descendant of Pygmalion and his statue.[11] Moreover, since Myrrha had already been transformed into a tree when she gave birth to Adonis, it would be technically correct to describe him as "of no woman bred" (rather like Macduff who is "of no woman born," *Macbeth*, V. x. 31); but one may doubt whether Venus is consciously using Adonis' extraordinary origins as a reproach. It is not his inhuman birth, but his unmanly behavior that worries her.

> "Thou art no man, though of a man's complexion,
> For men will kiss even by their own direction."
> (215–16)

The feminine rhymes underline the point, but the issue is complicated by his "man's complexion." In Elizabethan usage "complexion" could mean either "external appearance" or "natural disposition." The former sense would contradict Venus' presentation of his beauty as essentially

---

[11] In Ovid the union of Pygmalion and his statue produces a daughter, Paphos, who is the mother of Cinyras. Adonis, as fruit of the incestuous relation between Cinyras and Myrrha, is both the great and great-great grandson of a statue.

feminine (6–10); the latter is ruled out by his behavior. Perhaps we should gloss "man's complexion" as "possessing the defining physical attribute of a man," the unused "thing" that makes him "like a man." The ambiguities of "complexion" derive from and reinforce all the sexual confusions of the poem.

When Venus pauses (having spoken all but two of the last twenty stanzas), it is not because she has run out of arguments, but because "impatience chokes her pleading tongue" (217). The legal connotations of "pleading" lead on to "Being judge in love, she cannot right her cause" (220) which is only apparently paradoxical. It is, in fact, a statement of the basic principle that one cannot be both judge and plaintiff in the same case. Venus presides over the loves of mortals, but, as was implied by the Pygmalion allusion, she loses her power when she herself descends to love a mortal. The ambiguity of the preposition says it all: a judge who is in love can no longer be "judge in love." She is, indeed, worse off than any human judge, since there is no other judge to whom she can appeal: she is left without assistance precisely because the powers she has lost have been so absolute and undivided. The incompatibility between Venus in love and Venus as goddess of love is central to the poem's finely-calculated stance and effect. Though it creates opportunities for iconoclastic comedy in Ovid's Arachnean vein, it also gives her predicament an extra dimension of poignancy and pathos. The pathos will increase as the poem proceeds; but, as I have argued in the first chapter, our awareness that Venus is, after all, a goddess places a limit on our sympathy and blocks any final movement from the pathetic to the tragic.

Venus has, momentarily, lost command of speech ("her sobs do her intendments break," 222) and the syntax of the narrator mirrors her growing confusion. We start with an orderly sequence of anaphora ("And now ... and now," 221-22) and proceed to zeugma:

> Sometimes she shakes her head, and then his hand,
> Now gazeth she on him, now on the ground.
> (223–24)

But when, instead of one verb in the active voice governing two complements, we have a verb in the passive with two subjects, the picture becomes blurred: "She would, he will not in her arms be bound" (226). The ellipsis is brilliantly awkward—almost an aposiopesis, as if Venus' attempt to be bound in *his* arms had been interrupted by his refusal to be bound in hers. Much the same effect is created by "She locks her lily fingers one in one" (228) where "*his* lily fingers" would have made more obvious sense. The general impression is of a physical struggle so confused that the spectator-narrator has some difficulty sorting out who is doing what to whom.

The locking of fingers is an appropriate image for the deadlocked situation from which Venus, punning on "deer" and "pale," attempts to escape with a comic-erotic excursion on her own body as a deer-park.[12]

> "Fondling," she saith, "since I have hemmed thee here
> Within the circuit of this ivory pale,
> I'll be a park and thou shalt be my deer.
> Feed where thou wilt, on mountain or in dale;
>   Graze on my lips, and if those hills be dry,
>   Stray lower, where the pleasant fountains lie.
>
> "Within this limit is relief enough,
> Sweet bottom-grass and high delightful plain,
> Round rising hillocks, brakes obscure and rough,
> To shelter thee from tempest and from rain.
>   Then be my deer, since I am such a park;
>   No dog shall rouse thee, though a thousand bark."

---

[12] There is a perceptive discussion of the deer-park stanzas in Dubrow, 21–24.

In the mouth of a male speaker (Donne, "Elegy: To his Mistress Going to Bed") such a metaphor would have an imperialist ring since the woman's body almost inevitably becomes "virgin territory" to be discovered, penetrated and implanted. Venus, however, subverts these associations by presenting her own body as more like a nature-reserve where the native fauna, far from being hunted down, are given sustenance and protection. The significance of this move can be related to the way in which most Renaissance *epyllia* (especially Italian versions of the Venus and Adonis story) expand on the setting as a *locus amoenus*, a privileged site of libidinal freedom where a fruitful and harmonious nature encourages the satisfaction of sexual desire. Shakespeare does not allow his setting to function in such a simple way. He responds to the darker side of the *Metamorphoses* where, as Charles Segal observes, the landscape symbolizes "not only an inner world of free desires, but also a mysterious outer world where men meet an unwelcome and unexpected fate."[13] It is this revision of the *locus amoenus* that makes Ovid's landscape so disturbing: "by transforming the locales which in the literary tradition are places of comfort and refuge from the harsher realities of life, Ovid leaves a world bare of protection and open at any moment to sudden arbitrary attack."[14] The same can be said of the setting in *Venus and Adonis* which contains not only the healthy sexual vigor of the horses (259–324) and the joyous song of the lark (853–58), but also the desperate flight of the hunted hare (673–708), the paralyzing fear of the snail (1033–36) and the sheer destructiveness of the boar. In this light, Venus' landscape metaphor can be seen as an extension of the invitation to "come and sit where never serpent hisses" (17). The body of Venus is not so much a reflection of the poem's natural setting as a substitute for it.

---

[13] Charles Segal, *Landscape in Ovid's Metamorphoses: A Study in the Transformation of a Literary Symbol* (Wiesbdaden, 1969), 15.

[14] Segal, 74.

The metaphoric topography of the body offers a near-complete catalogue of landscape features: hill, mountain, dale, plain, grassland, water, wilderness. The aim, like that of any satisfactory park, is to combine the sense of enclosure and refuge ("Within the circuit of this ivory pale," "No dog shall rouse thee") with that of variety and freedom of choice ("Feed where thou wilt")—a blend neatly encapsulated in the double sense of "relief" ("Within this limit is relief enough"). Venus is offering Adonis a safer landscape than the one in which he wants to hunt. She may, however, suspect that Adonis regards the female anatomy as an even more perilous wilderness. She needs to re-present that anatomy in unthreatening terms and thus her metaphor involves a double substitution—for the real landscape around them and also for her own real body. Both the real landscape and the real body are dangerous: only the landscaped body is safe.

It is a brave attempt, but there are aspects of the metaphor that Adonis is unlikely to appreciate. It is all very well for Venus to abolish hunting within the limits of the park, but one doubts whether Adonis will be reassured by his transformation from hunter into deer. Even as a protected deer he still becomes a potential Actaeon threatened by his own dogs who bark outside the pale. From another angle, if Adonis sees hunting as a demonstration of virility, the goddess might have done better to develop the imperialist connotations of her landscape metaphor or to strengthen rather than dislocate the analogy between love and hunting. In the double sense of "venery" as both "the practice of hunting" and "the pursuit of sexual pleasure" the situation offers one obvious pun that Venus, despite her name, significantly fails to pick up. Her problem is that she cannot extend her protection to Adonis without at the same time reaffirming (as in the Mars-Venus passage) an emasculating female dominance. Her verbal energy in expanding her body into a landscape is somewhat analogous to the access of strength that allowed her to tuck Adonis under her arm. Rather than indicating any real area of freedom for the youth, it suggests the difficulty of finding any space that she has not already occupied.

The reader is not Adonis and need not share his presumed reservations. It is notoriously difficult to define what in literature functions as the erotic, but one suspects that this passage succeeds with the audience outside the poem, even if it fails to impress its addressee. And only the male reader who shares Ruskin's horror of pubic hair will find the topographical details detumescent. Since rhetoric is the medium that allows them to exist, almost all Shakespeare's characters are eloquent in one way or another; but Venus is one of those figures (like Richard II or Falstaff) in whom eloquence itself becomes a character trait—especially because her readiness to seize on each and every occasion for verbal fireworks stands in such marked contrast to the taciturnity of Adonis. Some readers have noted the absence of nudity in *Venus and Adonis*, but the eloquence of the goddess is already a form of self-exposure. To speak as much as she does is to lay oneself open to the world. In *Hero and Leander* the wide sleeves of Hero's garment show

> Where Venus in her naked glory strove
> To please the careless and disdainful eyes
> Of proud Adonis that before her lies.
> (*HL*, I. 12–14)

The "naked glory" of Shakespeare's Venus lies in the uninhibited, unashamed quality of her rhetorical display, a form of nudity that has its own erotic impact. It would, in any case, be churlish not to admire the goddess's achievement in reclaiming for women the discourse of desire usually reserved for men. One can see why a feminist philosopher like Michèle Le Doeuff goes so far as to argue that Venus is more interested in the language of love than in the fusion of bodies and that she finds a special jubilation in the freedom to deploy her creative imagination over the void created by the silence of Adonis.[15]

---

[15] Michèle Le Doeuff, *Vénus et Adonis suivi de Genèse d'une catastrophe* (Paris, 1986), 81.

One may doubt, however, whether Venus herself sees it this way. If it is the absence of the mistress that grants the Petrarchan lover-poet his imaginative freedom, then the concrete presence of Adonis in the poem works in the opposite direction so that we (and Venus) are constantly reminded that the verbal expression of desire is a very problematic substitute for its physical satisfaction. The very fact that the words of Venus so often excite her into gesture should be enough to show that, in her case, language does not create a self-sufficient world.

Venus has at least added another string to her rhetorical bow: we have already admired her dazzling switches from flattery to self-advertisement and from pleading to reproachful moralizing. Now she has tried humor and, for the first time, we are invited to laugh with Venus rather than at her. Even Adonis manages a smile and it takes only this hint of a positive response for Venus to lose her precarious comic-erotic poise in a welter of excitement provoked by his dimples. Despite the timely warning of a colleague who reminds me that a woman may admire a man's dimples without confusion of genders, it still strikes me that the narrator's imagery involves a remarkable change of perspective. So far we have been given the impression of an enveloping female body that threatens to absorb Adonis. Now it is the body of Adonis that offers "lovely caves," "enchanting pits" and, most strongly, "mouths to swallow Venus' liking" (247–48) in an inversion that confirms the ambiguous nature of Venus' desire. At the same time there is a proleptic touch of funereal imagery:

> Love made those hollows, if himself were slain,
> He might be buried in a tomb so simple,
>   Foreknowing well, if there he came to lie,
>   Why there love lived, and there he could not die.
>   (243–46)

The conceit foreshadows "What is thy body but a swallowing grave" (757) just as it echoes "the world hath ending with thy life" (12). Either this is something like free indirect speech or the narrator's sympathy with Venus has become so great that he cannot help imitating her hyperboles.

The narrator's increasing lack of distance culminates in Venus being directly addressed: "Poor queen of love, in thine own law forlorn" (251). This insertion of the second-person into a third-person narrative is analogous to the poem's alternation between past and present tense, avoiding the monotony of an unchanging narrative situation and maintaining a tension between sympathy and detachment, proximity and distance. The line recalls "Being judge in love, she cannot right her cause" (220) and pushes the implications a stage further. Venus is not merely a judge who is barred from applying the law to her own case, but a monarch who becomes a victim of the laws she has made for others—those laws dictating the pains of love that she will announce, as if she had just discovered them, at the end of the poem.

With the questions, "Now which way shall she turn? What shall she say?" (253–54), it might seem that we have a return to indirect free speech, but we can also see them as a genuine address to the reader who is invited to speculate on the development of a situation that has clearly reached an impasse. The suggestion is that the end may be imminent:

> Her words are done, her woes the more increasing.
> The time is spent; her object will away,
> And from her twining arms doth urge releasing.
> (254–56)

Shakespeare does, indeed, tempt us with the idea that Adonis has broken free ("Away he springs, and hasteth to his horse"), but his final escape will be delayed for another 550 lines. What is an impasse for the goddess need not be one for the poet.

One way out of a narrative impasse is to suddenly change the subject, but in such a way as to enable an eventual return to the old theme from a new angle. This is what Shakespeare does with the ecphrasis of the horses (259–324). Though it has no source in the *Metamorphoses*, the episode is structurally analogous to the insert-story of Hippomenes and Atalanta with which Ovid interrupts his account of Venus and Adonis.[16] What matters is the way Shakespeare integrates his ecphrasis into the movement and argument of the poem.

The first impression is one of welcome spatial contrast. So far the emphasis has been on immobility—Adonis as a bird in a net, bound in the arms of Venus or locked in her "lily fingers." Except for Venus' metaphorical expansion of her body, we have not moved from the spot where the struggle takes place. Now we are given a real not metaphorical space over which the horses range "outstripping crows." We would not expect a bridle fastened by the goddess of love (37–38) to be very effective in keeping the palfrey from the mare, and it is lucky for her that the courser "breaketh his rein" (264) just when Adonis succeeds in springing away. The result is a neat contrast between two simultaneous escapes, Adonis seeking freedom from love and the courser seeking freedom to love. As an image of powerful sexuality, the courser and the jennet provide an ironic slant on the earlier episode of Mars and Venus. In the "strong-necked steed" (263) with his "compassed crest" (272) there are unmistakable echoes of the god's "sinewy neck"(99) and "uncontrollèd crest" (104). But whereas Mars was rendered effeminate by his subjection to Venus, the masculinity of the horse is reinforced with imagery that abounds in suggestions of penetrative energy and phallic pride—the "hard hoof" wounding the "hollow womb" of the "bearing earth," the "ears up-pricked," the hairs

---

[16] Shakespeare may have remembered the horse as an image for sexual energy in the *Ars Amatoria* (I. 280 and II. 487) and there is a possible echo of *Hero and Leander* (II. 141–45):

> For as a hot proud horse highly disdains
> To have his head controlled, but breaks the reins,
> Spits forth the ringled bit, and with his hooves
> Checks the submissive ground: so he that loves,
> The more he is restrained, the worse he fares.

that "stand on end" (265–76). Venus taught Mars "to sport and dance, / To toy, to wanton, dally, smile, and jest" (105–06); the effect of desire on the courser is subtly but clearly different:

> Sometimes he trots, as if he told the steps,
> With gentle majesty and modest pride,
> Anon he rears upright, curvets and leaps,
> As who should say, Lo, thus my strength is tried.
> (277–80)

The courser in love maintains a male dignity that Venus had denied to Mars, "led prisoner in a red-rose chain" (110), or to Adonis as a pet in her deer-park.

The ecphrasis has, predictably, received sharply contrasting interpretations from readers who insist on taking sides. Those who blame Adonis for his reluctance to procreate follow Venus in seeing the courser as a model of healthy sexuality which Adonis would do well to imitate (403–08). Those who reproach Venus for her lust point to the couplet

> Look what a horse should have he did not lack,
> Save a proud rider on so proud a back.
> (299–300)

as implying that the courser represents appetite uncontrolled by reason—natural enough in an animal, but bestial in a man. The ecphrasis of the horses is thus even more ambivalent than the Mars-Venus episode and, though Shakespeare may be teasing us with these two incompatible readings, his poem supports neither of them. What is ultimately called into question is the whole idea of animal behavior as something from which human beings can draw a useful lesson, whether positive or negative. If, for example, the courser represents uncontrolled appetite, then we should, by a logical application of the metaphor, condemn Adonis as the "proud rider" who has lost control. But this makes no sense in view of Adonis' resistance to Venus. On the other hand, even more problems are raised by Venus' attempt to use the horses as an example of healthy uninhibited sexual energy. The horses do not, after all, go to it pell-mell. The courser first stages an elaborate exhibition of his own pride and power "to captivate the eye, / Of the fair breeder that is standing by" (281–82), but the jennet "puts on outward strangeness" (310); only when the courser assumes the air of a "melancholy malcontent" (313) does she finally relent and agree to his embrace. This sophisticated ritual of courtship undermines the goddess's argument that the horses provide a positive example of "natural" behavior. One might still argue (as Venus will) that the horses follow a natural pattern insofar as it is the male who takes the initiative; but in that case it is Venus herself who has made the model inapplicable and continues to do so in the very act of recommending it. The fact is that the horses only confirm conventional gender roles and thus offer no solution to the conflict of Venus and Adonis. Venus could, perhaps, have argued that, since she has already taken over the role of the courser, Adonis should imitate the jennet and yield after an initial display of coyness. This, however, is a line she does not take. For all her feminizing of Adonis, there are, it seems, limits to her freedom from convention and she cannot quite accept the inversion of gender roles that she herself has created. The point of the ecphrasis turns out, in the end, to be its inapplicability to the matter in hand. Nature tempts us with simple solutions that we are constitutionally incapable of imitating. There is ultimately no point in discussing whether Adonis should or should not follow the example of the courser. There is a gap fixed between man and animal and this (*pace* Desmond Morris) is particularly true when it comes to sexual behavior. The horses, even in their parody of human courtship, represent a sexual situation too simple to be of any relevance to the complex motivations of Venus and Adonis.

I have followed Clark Hulse in calling the episode of the horses an ecphrasis insofar as it is a self-contained piece of verbal painting.[17] It involves two separate rivalries: the first between nature and art as creators of beauty and the second between poetry and painting as representations of nature. In the late Renaissance the idea of nature as an aspiring artist, with all its implications for the theory of *mimesis*, is an inexhaustible source for the virtuosities of paradox, oxymoron, analogy and antithesis. One thinks of Spenser's Bower of Bliss (*FQ*, II. xii) and even more of Spenser's source in Tasso's description of Armida's garden:

> Stimi (sì misto il culto è co 'l negletto)
> Sol naturali e gli ornamenti e i siti.
> Di natura arte par, che per diletto
> L'imitatrice sua scherzando imiti.
>   (*Gerusalemme Liberata*, XVI. x)

> So with the rude the polished mingled was,
> That natural seemed all, and every part.
> Nature would craft in counterfeiting pass,
> And imitate her imitator art.
>   (tr. Edward Fairfax)

In the ecphrasis of the horses we find the same conceit that nature is at its finest when it seems to imitate the art that imitates nature.[18]

> Look when a painter would surpass the life
> In limning out a well proportioned steed,
> His art with nature's workmanship at strife,
> As if the dead the living should exceed:

---

[17] Clark Hulse, *Metamorphic Verse; The Elizabethan Minor Epic* (Princeton, NJ, 1981).

[18] In *The Winter's Tale* Shakespeare will finally collapse the distinction when Polixenes, answering Perdita's objection to hybrid flowers as unnatural ("nature's bastards"), argues that "The art itself is nature" (IV. iv. 97).

> So did this horse excel a common one
> In shape, in courage, colour, pace, and bone.
> (289–94)

High praise for the painter until we remember that this horse is, after all, the creation of a poet. Thus, in ascending order, we get nature's common horse, the painter's ideal horse, nature's ideal horse and finally the poet's horse. It is in this light that we need to read the detailed anatomical description:

> Round-hoofed, short-jointed, fetlocks shag and long,
> Broad breast, full eye, small head, and nostril wide,
> High crest, short ears, straight legs, and passing strong;
> Thin mane, thick tail, broad buttock, tender hide.
> (295–98)

The passage, which could have been derived from any number of contemporary treatises on horsemanship, has been attacked as "a paragraph from an advertisement of a horse sale" or "the minute self-defeating realism of the tyro."[19] But this is, perhaps, the very point that Shakespeare wants to make. There is more than a hint of parody in the detailed catalogue of all those aspects of a horse that a painter could hope to observe and reproduce. Our attention is drawn to the fact that painting, as a spatial art, is essentially static and can only give us a "lifeless picture." It takes the poet, as Shakespeare now demonstrates, to make the picture move:

---

[19] Edward Dowden, *Shakspere: A Critical Study of his Mind and Art* (London, 1875), 51. Bush, 146. Pauline Kiernan makes the interesting point that this demonstration that "a horse is a horse is a horse" stands in contrast to the rhetorical tropes of Venus who "succeeds only in saying that Adonis is everything but *himself.*" Pauline Kiernan, "Death by Rhetorical Trope: Poetry Metamorphosed in *Venus and Adonis* and the Sonnets," *RES* 46 (1995), 475–501 (p. 490).

> Sometimes he scuds far off, and there he stares;
> Anon he starts at stirring of a feather.
> To bid the wind a base he now prepares,
> And whe'er he run or fly they know not whether;
> > For through his mane and tail the high wind sings,
> > Fanning the hairs, who wave like feathered wings.
> > > (301–06)

Art and nature may struggle for supremacy, but in the competition between poet and painter there is little doubt about whom Shakespeare expects us to regard as the winner.

Adonis' pretentions as a hunter are obviously damaged by an episode where he loses control of his courser, and he returns "All swoll'n with chafing" (325)—a phrase that ironically suggests the reaction that the friction applied by Venus will fail to produce. We are set for another bout of courtship and the narrator drops a teasing hint that this time Venus may succeed ("lovesick love by pleading may be blessed," 328). And even if the blessing is not finally obtained, there will still be some relief in being able to plead.

> An oven that is stopped, or river stayed,
> Burneth more hotly, swelleth with more rage.
> So of concealèd sorrow may be said
> Free vent of words love's fire doth assuage.
> > But when the heart's attorney once is mute,
> > The client breaks as desperate in his suit.
> > > (331–36)

We have already seen the overflowing river (71–72) and the combination of water and fire (91–96); the recurrence of these images reminds us that Venus, despite the narrator's apparent optimism, is no nearer her goal. The return to an impasse is confirmed when, as Venus approaches, Adonis glows like "a dying coal" (338), an image that, taken with the stopped oven, creates an antagonistic balance (fire fighting fire) between his chastity and her desire. The narrator's optimistic metaphors turn out to be misleading. Venus' "free vent of words," far from assuaging "love's fire," will only increase it. In her case "the heart's attorney" never will be mute, but the client will go bankrupt just the same. The narrator tells us that hope cannot survive the loss of speech; what the poem demonstrates is that speech survives the loss of hope.

It is striking that at this stage, when the narrator seems anything but omniscient, he should suddenly switch from the present to the past tense: "O, what a sight it was wistly to view / How she came stealing to the wayward boy" (343-44). We are abruptly reminded that what sounds like a running commentary is, in fact, a reconstruction and that, therefore, the narrator must know how the story will end. There is, perhaps, a subliminal hint of what that ending will be as Adonis "looks on the dull earth" (340) that is soon to receive him. In one sense at least the chaste Adonis will prove more earthy than the sensual goddess.

The heat that preceded the ecphrasis of the horses has now given way to a climate that is both more temperate and more promising. As if to augur some ideal mutuality in love, the adjectives move freely between Venus and Adonis: her "fair hand" and "his fair cheek," "Her other tender hand" and "His tend'rer cheek" (351-53). Even the virginal image of snow is here exploited for its receptive quality rather than its coldness:

> His tend'rer cheek receives her soft hand's print,
> As apt as new-fall'n snow takes any dint.
> (353-54)

These hints of reconciliation are not really contradicted by the subsequent "war of looks;" the patterning becomes so excessively neat that one gets the impression of an obligatory ritual rather than a genuine conflict.

> O, what a war of looks was then between them,
> Her eyes petitioners to his eyes suing!
> His eyes saw her eyes as they had not seen them;

> Her eyes wooed still; his eyes disdained the wooing;
> And all this dumb play had his acts made plain
> With tears which, chorus-like, her eyes did rain.
>   (355–60)

This is one of the rare passages where, for this reader at least, the rhetoric of *Venus and Adonis* falls flat. The antimetabole ("her eyes – his eyes – his eyes – her eyes") comes too soon after the same pattern in the previous stanza ("hand – cheek – cheek – hand") and is then extended by a further sequence of "her eyes – his eyes – her eyes" as if the rhetorical figure in itself had become a mere automatism. Moreover, the theatrical metaphor of the couplet simply does not work out: since both looks and tears are non-verbal signs, it is hard to see how one can serve as a chorus to explain the "dumb play" of the other.

The temporary lapse is immediately and amply redeemed when we return from looks to gesture.

> Full gently now she takes him by the hand,
> A lily prisoned in a jail of snow,
> Or ivory in an alabaster band;
> So white a friend engirds so white a foe.
>   This beauteous combat, wilful and unwilling,
>   Showed like two silver doves that sit a-billing.
>   (361–66)

The images of lily, snow, ivory and alabaster indicate not only a shared whiteness but also a shared blend of hardness and softness. What gives the passage its unexpected subtlety is that the hard-soft antitheses point not to the contrast between the protagonists but to the combination of beauty and inflexibility that they have in common: the hand of Adonis is both lily and ivory, that of Venus both snow and alabaster. At the same time, one recognizes that ivory and alabaster do not have perfectly identical connotations: ivory suggests the delicate and finely-carved epicene beauty of Adonis; alabaster the more imposing, large-scale quality of Venus. The blend of hard and soft is carried through to the "silver doves" of the couplet, but already the verb "showed" threatens the idyllic interlude. Appearances are deceptive and the fragile aesthetic harmony created by the imagery does not herald a resolution of the conflict.

The silence is, predictably, broken by Venus who, imagining an exchange of biological status, indulges in a vision of herself as dominant male generously condescending to assuage female desire.

> Once more the engine of her thoughts began:
> "O fairest mover on this mortal round,
> Would thou wert as I am, and I a man,
> My heart all whole as thine, thy heart my wound;
> For one sweet look thy help I would assure thee,
> Though nothing but my body's bane would cure thee."
> (367–72)

The argument is pathetically disingenuous since we know that, if Venus wishes to be a man, it is not to offer help to some frustrated female Adonis, but because she wants the physical power to satisfy her own desire. And even here we see that she has difficulties in projecting herself into an unambiguously male role. Traditionally we think of the woman as being wounded (stabbed, pierced) in the act of love, but in Venus' version it is the male who risks his "body's bane" to satisfy the female. It is clearly too simple to see Venus as a woman who seeks to assume the male role, although her desire frequently emerges that way. Her real problem is that she wants all roles at once, a sexuality that defies both conventional gender patterns and the constraints of biology. It is not surprising that her rhetoric should occasionally tie itself in knots.

From gender exchange we come back to more familiar ground in the exchange of hands and hearts.

> "Give me my hand," saith he. "Why dost thou feel it?"
> "Give me my heart," saith she, "and thou shalt have it.

> O give it me, lest thy hard heart do steel it,
> And being steeled, soft sighs can never grave it.
> Then love's deep groans I never shall regard,
> Because Adonis' heart hath made mine hard."
> (373-78)

This resembles a distortion of the marriage ceremony where hearts and hands are given together. Adonis asks for the return of his hand and Venus demands in exchange the return of her heart. We might expect that Venus would want to repossess her heart in order to preserve it from the wounds of love, but, in a witty variation on the old motif, she insists that she needs her heart in order to maintain its vulnerability. She fears that the "hard heart" of Adonis will both "steal" and "steel" her own. It is not those who are in love but those who are incapable of loving who have truly lost their heart. And it is the immortal goddess not the mortal youth who now wears vulnerability as a badge of distinction.

Adonis protests with an antistasis, "let go, and let me go" (379), but then rather tactlessly focuses attention on the whole issue of sexuality and "natural" behavior by claiming that his sole concern is "how to get my palfrey from the mare" (384). It would be unlike Venus to let slip this golden occasion to revive the debate.

> Thus she replies: "Thy palfrey, as he should,
> Welcomes the warm approach of sweet desire.
> Affection is a coal that must be cooled,
> Else, suffered, it will set the heart on fire.
> The sea hath bounds, but deep desire hath none;
> Therefore no marvel though thy horse be gone."
> (385-90)

On the surface Venus is simply arguing that no imposed limits will prevent desire from seeking satisfaction. As persuasion this is unlikely to be effective since she is using the palfrey to define her own feelings rather than those of Adonis. Moreover, she passes from the initial statement that desire must be assuaged ("a coal that must be cooled") to an affirmation that desire knows no bounds—with the inevitable implication (already noted at 19–20) that it never can be assuaged. The awkwardness of presenting the courser as a model for Adonis becomes clear when she celebrates his escape from "petty bondage," conveniently forgetting that she has already boasted of chaining Mars (109–10) and is, at that very moment, confining Adonis in her arms. More promising as erotic incitement might be her account of how a real male reacts when he "sees his true-love in her naked bed" (397), but even here Venus manages to shoot herself in the foot with a last rhetorical flourish:

> "Who is so faint that dares not be so bold
> To touch the fire, the weather being cold?"
> (401–02)

The couplet has a delightfully colloquial and proverbial tone, rather like the modern litotes "I wouldn't kick her out of bed on a frosty night." But the attempt at meiosis, the suggestion that lovemaking need not be such a traumatic experience, stands at odds with the image itself. Adonis, who has already complained of sunburn (186), might reflect that "to touch the fire" will produce searing pain even in cold weather. All analogies have their limits and this is not the only occasion when Venus pushes a potentially persuasive metaphor to the point where it becomes counter-productive. "Though I were dumb, yet his proceedings teach thee" (406) exclaims the goddess, and we are reminded that it is her own rhetorical exuberance that ends by defeating the lesson it was intended to reinforce.

So far we have heard nothing from Adonis but petulant protest (185–86, 379–84). We now discover that he has a mind of his own and the unexpected capacity to mount a highly rhetorical assault, complete with ploke, antithesis, antimetabole and paradox.

> "I know not love," quoth he, "nor will not know it,
> Unless it be a boar, and then I chase it.

> 'Tis much to borrow, and I will not owe it.
> My love to love is love but to disgrace it;
> For I have heard it is a life in death,
> That laughs and weeps, and all but with a breath."
> (409–14)

It is no accident that Adonis' first speech on love should coincide with the poem's first mention of the boar. If, like Venus, we cannot imagine "love" without some form of physical penetration, then it is obviously true that Adonis "will not know it / Unless it be a boar." The boar's very name is proleptic in that he possesses the instruments to "bore" that Venus lacks.

In this sense it is fair enough to say that Adonis unwittingly announces the boar as a male rival of Venus. It is quite another thing to suggest that Adonis prefers the homosexual embrace of the boar to a heterosexual union with Venus.[20] Loving to hunt an animal is not the same as loving the animal that one hunts, whatever the field-sports lobby may say. The primary sense of "Unless it be a boar" is that Adonis places love and the boar in the same category as things he wants to "disgrace;" he wishes love would assume some form that he could hunt down and destroy.

Other details in the stanza reveal the motives underlying this categorical rejection of love. The metaphor of borrowing and owing suggests an adolescent fear of responsibility. Since "owe" can be glossed as "own" with the double sense of "recognize" and "possess," there is also the implication that Adonis refuses to recognize the rights of an emotion that involves a loss of self-possession. The couplet

---

[20] Though Adonis will later play on "know" in the sense of carnal knowledge ("Before I know myself, seek not to know me," 525), it may be doubted whether he is doing so here. Coppélia Kahn thinks there is "a glance at sodomy," but we should not confuse the feelings of Adonis with the desire he might arouse. See Coppélia Kahn, "Self and Eros in *Venus and Adonis,*" *Centennial Review* 4 (1976), 351–71 (p. 365).

conveys his horror of instability ("That laughs and weeps") or of anything that threatens his fragile autonomy. At "I have heard it is a life in death," we suspect that Adonis has slipped up and that he means "death in life;" but the lapse may be ironically significant since Adonis, doomed to die like all mortals, refuses the "life in death" that Venus has proclaimed as the purpose of procreative sex (169–74). Despite the dismissive and categorical tone, the whole stanza, with its crippling fear of knowing and owing, suggests how deeply Adonis is confused by the unsettling advent of adult experience.

Adonis' fear of being forced into maturity is made explicit when, remembering Venus' recognition of his unripeness and her dictum that flowers should be "gathered in their prime" (127–32), he argues that his own prime will be jeopardized if he surrenders:

> "Who wears a garment shapeless and unfinished?
> Who plucks the bud before one leaf put forth?
> If springing things be any jot diminished,
> They wither in their prime, prove nothing worth.
>   The colt that's backed and burdened being young,
>   Loseth his pride, and never waxeth strong."
>   (415–20)

The list culminates with the colt because Adonis seeks to establish a difference between himself and the courser and, at the same time, to use against Venus her own equine analogy. The phrase "backed and burdened" recalls the conventional riding metaphor for copulation, but also indicates its limits since, in this case, it involves putting a male (colt) in the passive role. "Prime" may well be contaminated by its adjectival use as a synonym for "lustful" ("as prime as goats," *Othello*, III. iii. 408) and still hovers between the senses of springtime and maturity—the idea being that if Venus wants to enjoy the sexual best of Adonis (his "pride") she should abstain from exploiting his youth. Adonis is both adept at defeating Venus with her own arguments and diplomatic in holding out the promise of some future satisfaction. He conveniently forgets (if he ever knew) that his unripeness is precisely what makes him attractive. Moreover, the reasoning of Adonis is scarcely more consistent than that of Venus since he follows up an outright rejection of love with the plea that he will be a better lover if given time to develop. We recognize the concession as more tactical than real when he immediately reverts to his dismissive tone.

> "Remove your siege from my unyielding heart;
> To love's alarms it will not ope the gate.
> Dismiss your vows, your feignèd tears, your flatt'ry;
> For where a heart is hard they make no batt'ry."
> (423–26)

It is Venus, we remember, who introduced military imagery into the poem with the account of her conquest over Mars (97–114). That imagery is now maliciously turned against her. We are reminded that, however politely Petrarchists may use the siege metaphor, its very existence testifies to the fact that men possess the physical means of assault (the battering ram) that women lack. The woman as besieger cannot really threaten to literalize her metaphor; the derisive feminine "flatt'ry – batt'ry" rhyme neatly conveys the scorn of an epigrammatic intelligence unmasking an elaborate pretense.

After his previous taciturnity, the eloquence of Adonis comes as such a surprise to Venus ("What, canst thou talk?," 427) that she sees it as inverting the whole situation. Far from weighing on Adonis, she becomes the one who is "pressed with bearing" (430); the temptress assumes the role of the tempted male, lured to destruction by a "mermaid's voice" (429) whose dangerous enticement can only be described with elaborate oxymoron:

> "Melodious discord, heavenly tune harsh-sounding,
> Ears' deep-sweet music, and heart's deep-sore wounding."
> (431–32)

Like the chiasmus and antimetabole which abound in *Venus and Adonis*, oxymoron is a typically Petrarchan figure precisely because it tends to block forward movement. Venus' attempt to break out of the impasse is signaled by her immediate recourse to the antidote of climax or gradatio with its orderly progression from one step to the next. In a passage of fourteen lines (433-46) she moves from sight to hearing, from hearing to touch, from touch to smell and finally from smell to taste. In the traditional hierarchy of the senses sight and hearing count as the superior and more spiritual—sight because it is metaphoric for intellectual vision, and hearing because, as Venus suggests, it gives access to "that inward beauty and invisible" (434).[21] Not for the first time, Venus descends the scale towards the earthy and immediate. We remember her description of the lover who proceeds from the "glutton eye" through the "other agents" until he is finally brought to "touch the fire" (397-402). Here, however, taking her cue from the Platonic metaphor of the banquet, she replaces touch with taste as the moment of what we must obviously call consummation.

> "But O, what banquet wert thou to the taste,
> Being nurse and feeder to the other four!
> Would they not wish the feast might ever last
> And bid suspicion double-lock the door
>   Lest jealousy, that sour unwelcome guest,
>   Should by his stealing-in disturb the feast?"
>   (445-50)

The substitution is perfectly in character, given the feeding metaphors that have accumulated around the invitations and assaults of Venus— the stuffed gorge of the eagle" (55-60), the "dainties to taste" (164), the youth's unripeness which may "well be tasted" (128) and his breath on which she feeds (63), to say nothing of the goddess's own "honey secrets" (16), her juiciness (136) and the park of her body where

---

[21] For a discussion of the hierarchy of the senses, see Frank Kermode, *Shakespeare, Spenser, Donne: Renaissance Essays* (London, 1971), Chapter 4, "The Banquet of Sense."

Adonis is invited to graze (229–34). With these recurrent images of feeding and orality the poem covers the whole range of Venus' "variable passions" so that we see her by turns as a sophisticated epicure offering strange refinements to the sexual appetite, as a healthy hedonist or a simple embodiment of nature's bounty, as a nurturing protective mother and as a devouring predator. As provider and consumer Venus is a "feeder" in two senses; but in her discourse the two senses appear to be mutually exclusive and the one metaphor to escape her is that of nutritional exchange.

The "jealousy" that threatens the banquet is not explicitly sexual and does not grow out of anything in the immediate context; it is rather the vague "apprehension of evil" (OED 5) likely to shadow any happiness that would otherwise be perfect. The reader may remember Adonis' mention of the boar (410), but there is no suggestion that Venus does so. Venus evokes a fear that she cannot define whereas the reader knows that the real danger has already been announced by the musical voice that enchants her.

As Adonis opens his mouth to interrupt the goddess, the narrator arrests the action to contemplate the "ruby-coloured portal" that yields "honey passage" to his speech (451–52). The imagery recalls the "honey secrets" (16) promised by Venus and the way the dimples of Adonis have already been transformed into "mouths to swallow Venus' liking" (248).[22] Once again it is the narrator's regard that suggests how Adonis unwittingly tempts Venus with the penetrative role that he has himself been offered and refused. The comparison of the red mouth to a threatening "red morn" (453) provides a distant gloss on the sunrise that opens the poem and initiates an anaphoric series of similes.

---

[22] Richard Barnfield probably remembers this passage in the blazoning of a homoerotic sonnet that begins by evoking "Cherry-lipped Adonis" as a term of comparison: "His lips ripe strawberries in nectar wet, / His mouth a hive, his tongue a honey-comb / Where Muses (like bees) make their mansion" (*Cynthia*, 1595).

> This ill presage advisedly she marketh.
> Even as the wind is hushed before it raineth,
> Or as the wolf doth grin before he barketh.
> Or as the berry breaks before it staineth,
> > Or like the deadly bullet of a gun,
> > His meaning struck her ere his words begun.
> > > (457–62)

There is a sureness of rhetorical touch in the way the homoioteleuton of the rhymes ("marketh," "raineth," "barketh," "staineth") is offset by varying verb forms in the first half of each simile ("is hushed," "doth grin," "breaks"). The order of the similes is by no means casual since there is a progressive reduction of the gap between warning sign and event until at last, with the bullet, the event overtakes the warning. If the action had seemed arrested with the opening mouth of Adonis, it is now speeded up until action and reaction become simultaneous.

Venus "flatly falleth down" (463) and the adverb is wonderfully apt, combining as it does the immediacy of her reaction, the position in which she falls and the sense of a deliberate gesture. Our suspicion that this is a tactical move designed to convert the regard of Adonis from hostility to sympathy is strengthened by the antimetabole "For looks kill love, and love by looks reviveth" (464), while the punning in "Fair fall the wit that can so well defend her!" (472) combines good wishes for the future with the sense of a fall that has already proved lucky by putting Venus in the position she seeks underneath Adonis. To all this Adonis reacts with the confused and panicky gestures that one would expect from someone who has no experience of fainting women. Only when he has tried a series of grotesque and violent gestures (clapping her cheek, wringing her nose, bending her fingers, (475–76) does he finally opt for the life-giving kiss. At "his breath breatheth life in her again" (474) we may remember Marlowe's Leander in a similar situation:

> By this, sad Hero, with love unacquainted,
> Viewing Leander's face, fell down and fainted.
> He kissed her, and breathed life into her lips.
> 			(*HL*, II. 1–3)

The comparison reveals all the difference between the bungling of Adonis and the prompt response of a true lover. Leander will proceed from kissing to a wrestling with Hero that revives "a gentle pleasing heat" and teaches him "all that elder lovers know" (II. 68–69); but Adonis, with his clapping, wringing, finger-bending and chafing, has already provided the friction supposedly required to arouse generative warmth in the cold female. By moving from friction to kissing he inverts the standard sequence of sexual stimulation, unwittingly exacerbating in the overheated goddess a demand that kissing is unlikely to satisfy. The friction which provides natural instruction for Marlowe's lovers serves no useful purpose in a situation where Adonis cannot be taught and Venus has nothing to learn.

The revival of Venus is accompanied by two stanzas of extraordinarily incoherent cosmic imagery (481–92). The eyes of Venus are seen first as "two blue windows" and then as a "fair sun;" added to those of Adonis they make "four such lamps" and finally they resemble the moon. With such shifting between singular and plural it sounds rather as if the narrator is suffering from the same derangement of vision that will later affect Venus (1063–68); but the passage finally emerges from confusion into the visual precision of "the moon in water seen by night" (492) which has that special semi-transparent quality that Shakespeare exploits so well.[23]

Venus recovers her voice to describe what sounds like an orgasm, but one suspects that she is using her rhetorical powers to transform

---

[23] Other examples in the poem would be "lawn being spread upon the blushing rose" (590), "pearls in glass" (980) and, given the faintly translucent quality of alabaster, "ivory in an alabaster band" (363).

into orgasm an experience that has fallen well short of it. Venus has argued so explicitly in favor of copulation that, even if we allow for the conventional raptures that the kiss usually inspires in Renaissance poetry, there is still a comic disproportion between the rhetoric and its occasion. Venus combines the usual antitheses (earth-heaven, ocean-fire, morning-evening) with her obsessive figures of oxymoron, chiasmus and antimetabole to work up to the inevitable death in life or "life in death" (413) that Adonis knows only by hearsay and now hears yet again.

> "But now I lived, and life was death's annoy,
> But now I died, and death was lively joy."
> (497–98)

The dominant figure continues to be antimetabole as the eyes of Adonis, tutored by his "hard heart," murder the "poor heart" of Venus which would be followed into death by her own loyal eyes ("true leaders to their queen") were it not for the action of his "piteous lips" (499–504), now celebrated for their life-preserving qualities.

> "Long may they kiss each other, for this cure!
> O, never let their crimson liveries wear,
> And, as they last, their verdure still endure
> To drive infection from the dangerous year,
>   That the star-gazers having writ on death,
>   May say the plague is banished by thy breath!"
> (505–10)

The "crimson liveries" continue the feudal metaphor introduced by the loyal eyes, but "cure" adds a medical motif. The bright red color of the lips is analogous to the fresh green of aromatic herbs used to ward off infection. The "dangerous year" may be that of the poem's composition (1592–93) when the plague was raging and the theaters were closed, or any year marked out in advance as inauspicious. As in Sonnet 107 where the proclamation of peace makes "the sad augurs mock their own presage," so here "the star-gazers" will be forced to revise their predictions and confirm that the plague has been banished by the breath of Adonis which has both the purifying quality of the wind and the absolute authority of a monarch.

The idea of purification and the sense of banishment as involving a formal proclamation under a royal seal provide a transition to "Pure lips, sweet seals" and to the imagery of law and commerce which, as in the *Sonnets*, Shakespeare exploits to present love as a transaction that defies business logic (511–16). If kisses are the seals of love ("Seals of love, though sealed in vain," *Measure*, IV. i. 1–6), then Venus is prepared to strike any number of bargains for the pleasure "still to be sealing." Since a "seal" can be either the wax on which the impression has been made or the instrument that makes the impression, the metaphor remains sexually ambiguous despite Venus' attempt to give Adonis the male role ("Set thy seal manual on my wax-red lips," 516). The "slips" against which the seal is a guarantee may be counterfeit coins, but we might also think of her fear that Adonis will try to slip out of the bargain. The whole metaphor has an inescapably comic dimension if we reflect that Venus, the champion of *copia*, is asking for her lips to be sealed.

The mobility that we have seen as characteristic of Venus' rhetoric allows the kisses to be both the seals on the contract and the payment that the contract imposes (517–22). The kiss-money metaphor is reinforced when the Catullan hyperbole of "a thousand kisses" is repeated as "ten hundred touches," linking the touch of lips to the "touch" that is the official stamp distinguishing legal tender from counterfeit "slips." When the thousand kisses become "twenty hundred" as a penalty for non-payment we may remember how Venus had promised that "one sweet kiss shall pay this countless debt" (84). Not even Falstaff in his most expansive mood could have imagined such an inflation. At this rate, the kiss will soon be worth considerably less than it was when it revived the goddess from her faint.

As if to deny that the episode of the kiss has modified the situation or that it represents any significant concession, Adonis replies by reverting to his old argument of unripeness.

> "Fair queen," quoth he, "if any love you owe me,
> Measure my strangeness with my unripe years.
> Before I know myself, seek not to know me.
> No fisher but the ungrown fry forbears.
>   The mellow plum doth fall, the green sticks fast,
>   Or, being early plucked, is sour to taste."
>   (523–28)

The first part of *Venus and Adonis* is structured in a way that could be described as spiral, repeating the same basic situations, but each time at a different level, with an ever-increasing degree of complexity and tension. Here, for instance, comparison with the earlier speech (409–26) reveals a considerable evolution. The argument is not preceded by any outright rejection of love or followed a boast of invincibility. Adonis addresses Venus with courtesy ("Fair queen") and seems ready to accord her love some serious attention, at least as a hypothesis ("if any love you owe me"). He then elevates the discussion by linking the physical and the psychological, carnal knowledge with self-knowledge. We may recognize the limitations of the argument and its relation to the illusory self-sufficiency condemned in the *Sonnets*, but that does not mean that it can be easily dismissed. *Nosce teipsum* was, after all, a standard Renaissance injunction to moral development and Adonis speaks with a massive weight of tradition on his side. Moreover, if Adonis refuses to grow towards the Other (like those "who moving others are themselves as stone," Sonnet 94), it must be said that Venus, with her physical aggression and verbal dominance, leaves him little space for such growth. If Adonis denies the Other by retreating into his shell, Venus also denies the Other by her invasiveness. It is, in any case, impossible to know how much self-knowledge is needed to make that encounter with the Other fruitful rather than destructive. Hence the element of risk associated with the first sexual experience. Not for nothing does Ovid so often link sudden sexual initiation with a metamorphosis that destroys human identity. Adonis' belief that self-knowledge should precede carnal knowledge is no more naive than Venus' conviction that sex is necessarily simple and healthy.

Adonis, by pleading his unripeness, is playing for time; and time seems to be on his side since it has brought him relatively unscathed to the end of the day (529-34). The imagery, by reminding us that that other creatures (the owl, birds, sheep) inhabit the landscape and by setting the action against the broad backdrop of the sky ("coal-black clouds, that shadow heaven's light"), offers a respite from the narrow focus on the protagonists. Nature, however, is deceptive in its promises of conclusion: Adonis will have to struggle again before he can follow the animals to rest; the sun's "hot task" is over, but for Venus the greatest heat is yet to come. As we should have learned from the episode of the horses, the human rhythms of Venus and Adonis are not geared to those of the natural world.

Taking advantage of the restful atmosphere and wisely ignoring the inflationary "thousand kisses," Adonis now takes Venus up on her original promises and offers a single kiss in exchange for the "good night" that will signal his release (535-36). It is a crucial moment in the poem. A sexual gesture is freely made and accepted: for one fleeting instant we are offered a vision of what might have been.

> The honey fee of parting tendered is.
> Her arms do lend his neck a sweet embrace.
> Incorporate then they seem; face grows to face.
> (538-40)

The honey that Venus promised as an enticement to capture Adonis (15-16) is now granted by Adonis himself as a fee to purchase his freedom. "Tendered" continues the monetary metaphor (legal tender), but also gathers up the two adjectival senses of "tender" as youthful and affectionate. In Adonis those two senses have so far proved incompatible (see "So young and so untender," *Lear* F, I. i. 106); here, it seems, they coincide for the first and only time. A rhyming echo confirms the impression of a perfectly-balanced exchange when the arms of Venus "lend" an embrace in response to the "*tend*ered" kiss of Adonis. The resulting fusion of bodies recalls Ovid's story of Salmacis and Hermaphroditus where, as in *Venus and Adonis*, an infatuated woman pursues a reluctant and beautiful youth. When Salmacis, overcome by the sight of Hermaphroditus bathing naked in a pool, wades in and embraces him, the gods, in answer to her prayer, merge the two bodies into an androgynous figure.

> nam mixta duorum
> corpora iunguntur, faciesque inducitur illis
> una. velut, si quis conducat cortice ramos,
> crescendo iungi pariterque adolescere cernit,
> sic ubi conplexu coierunt membra tenaci,
> nec duo sunt et forma duplex, nec femina dici
> nec puer ut possit, neutrumque et utrumque videntur.
> (*Met*, IV. 373–79)

For their two bodies, joined together as they were, were merged in one, with one face and form for both. As when one grafts a twig on some tree, he sees the branches grow one, and with common life come to maturity, so were these two bodies knit in a close embrace: they were no longer two, nor such as to be called, one, woman, and one, man. They seemed neither, and yet both.

Since Ovid, in etiological fashion, concludes that henceforth any man who enters that pool will emerge enfeebled and transformed into a hermaphrodite, the story could be read, as it was by *Ovide moralisé* and by Golding, as a dreadful warning against effeminacy.[24] And yet,

---

[24] *Ovide moralisé* (IV. 2224–2389) uses the story as a warning to monks who venture too far from their cloister. Bersuire had responded more positively since he reads the tale as an allegory of the union of human and divine natures in Christ. *Metamorphosis Ovidiana Moraliter Explanata* (Paris, 1509), f.xl.

although official Renaissance thought certainly maintained what Linda Woodbridge calls "a tradition of fear and contempt for physical androgyny,"[25] the hermaphrodite as a literary image could be marvelous as well as monstrous. Jonathan Bate is surely right when he argues that in Ovid the moment of metamorphic union "suggests not halving of strength but doubling of perfection" and that this "is an image of how sex should be."[26] Such a reading is not necessarily the product of our twentieth-century recognition of bisexuality; Plato's *Symposium* had already entertained the view that man seeks through sexual intercourse the restoration of an original and ideal bisexual identity. That the Neoplatonic Renaissance also could see in the hermaphrodite the image of complete sexual fulfillment is suggested by Donne:

> So to one neutral thing both sexes fit.
> We die and rise the same, and prove
> Mysterious by this love.
> ("The Canonization")

and even more strongly by Spenser when Britomart witnesses the embrace between Amoret and Scudamour:

> Had ye them seen, ye would have surely thought
> That they had been that fair hermaphrodite
> Which that rich Roman of white marble wrought,
> And in his costly bath caused to be site:
> So seemed those two, as grown together quite,
> That Britomart half envying their bless,
> Was much empassioned in her gentle sprite,
> And to herself oft wished like happiness.
> (*FQ*, III. xii. st. 46. 1590 version)

---

[25] Linda Woodbridge, *Women and the English Renaissance. Literature and the Nature of Womankind, 1520–1620* (Brighton, 1984), 141.

[26] Bate, 62.

The hermaphrodite figure is particularly relevant to *Venus and Adonis* because we already think of both protagonists in bisexual terms— Adonis as a hunter, proud of his male autonomy and yet feminine in his beauty and virginally fearful of sexual invasion; Venus as a woman inviting penetration, yet attracted by a beauty that, with its enticing hollows, casts her in the male role. What could be more fitting than that one doubly sexual identity should replace two split sexual identities and that sexual fusion should be the answer to sexual confusion.

The image is too perfect to last: "Incorporate then they seem," but incorporate they are not. A rapid return to the feeding metaphor (541–46) shows how Venus and Adonis emerge unmodified from the kiss. For Venus too much ("surfeit") is not enough, and for Adonis enough ("plenty") is already too much. Once again they "fall to the earth" and it is, indeed, a fall back from the vision of ungendered harmony into the familiar pattern of aggression and resistance. The "heavenly moisture" offered by Adonis provokes a very earthy appetite.[27]

> Now quick desire hath caught the yielding prey,
> And glutton-like she feeds, yet never filleth.
> Her lips are conquerors, his lips obey,
> Paying what ransom the insulter willeth,
>
> > Whose vulture thought doth pitch the price so high
> > That she will draw his lips' rich treasure dry.
> >
> > (547–52)

---

[27] The analogous passage in Fraunce is enough to show that cosmological readings of the myth did not exclude heavy-handed attempts at eroticism: "And then Adonis lipps with her owne lipps kindely she kisseth, / Rolling tongue, moyst mouth with her owne mouth to be sucking, / Mouth and tong and lipps, with Ioves drinck Nectar abounding" (*Yvychurch*, 44).

The images of violence return, but with further degradation as the "empty eagle" (55) is replaced by the more repulsive vulture. As for the siege metaphor, even the brutal conventions of warfare are not enough to satisfy the goddess who, not content with ransom, descends to indiscriminate looting.

> And, having felt the sweetness of the spoil,
> With blindfold fury she begins to forage.
> Her face doth reek and smoke, her blood doth boil,
> And careless lust stirs up a desperate courage,
>   Planting oblivion, beating reason back,
>   Forgetting shame's pure blush and honour's wrack.
>   (553–58)

The extended metaphor leaves the reader free to imagine the details of the sexual assault, but we surely know this narrator too well to take his finger-wagging couplet entirely seriously. The following stanza immediately dissipates any feeling of moral outrage.

> Hot, faint, and weary with her hard embracing,
> Like a wild bird being tamed with too much handling,
> Or as the fleet-foot roe that's tired with chasing,
> Or like the froward infant stilled with dandling,
>   He now obeys, and now no more resisteth,
>   While she takes all she can, not all she listeth.
>   (559–64)

That this temporary victory does not take Venus much further than the old stalemate is suggested by the repetition of some familiar effects. The tired heat of Adonis stands in contrast to the sexual heat of Venus just as it did earlier when he was compared to "a dying coal" and she to "an oven that is stopped" (331–38). Adonis has already been seen as a captured bird (67) after the "empty eagle" stanza (55–60) and here again an almost identical image conveys the same sense of sympathy for the youth while redimensioning the violence to which he has been subjected. The final simile, by replacing "handling" with "dandling," completes the process by reducing what had looked like serious physical aggression to a gesture of maternal solicitude towards a fretful child.

At this stage the poem seems to hover between a predatory and a maternal Venus, and the narrator cannot be relied on to provide a stable perspective. The behavior that he has just castigated as an affront to reason, shame and honor he now recommends as the lover's path to success (565–76). Remembering Venus' image of the seal (511–16), he inverts its application in order to restore the initiative to the goddess: it is no longer the wax-red lips" of Venus that will be "imprinted" by Adonis, but his frozen wax, dissolved by her tempering heat, that will yield "to every light impression." Venus has attempted to take far more than the single kiss stipulated in the bargain offered by Adonis, but this piece of sharp practice is commendable since no contract can impose terms on love "whose leave exceeds commission." That Venus has fixed her desire on a seemingly impossible object is also turned to her advantage:

> Affection faints not, like a pale-faced coward,
> But then woos best when most his choice is froward.
> (569–70)

Since Adonis has just been compared to a "froward infant," this might seem to make the simple point that a lover should not be discouraged by resistance; but there is also the glimpse of a connection between rhetoric and perversity, a hint that the rhetoric of Venus (when she "woos best") would excite less admiration if her choice were not so contrary to reason and morality. In this light, the justification of any given desire would lie not in some intrinsically fitting quality of the desired object but in the quality of the discourse it provokes.

We may admire the means; Venus herself is more concerned with the end. "Words pay no debts, give her deeds" as Pandarus would say (*Troilus*, III. ii. 53). Her persistence has already won the "nectar" of

Adonis' lips and the narrator sees in this a good omen for her final conquest of his virginity.

> Foul words and frowns must not repel a lover.
> What though the rose have prickles, yet 'tis plucked!
>   Were beauty under twenty locks kept fast,
>   Yet love breaks through, and picks them all at last.
>   (573–76)

One suspects a form of indirect free speech. Once again, the narrator is so absorbed in the scene he has recreated that he can give voice to Venus' unspoken thoughts and, for a moment, share her ignorance of the future.

It is typical of a poem that delights in creating and frustrating expectations that we now get what might be called a double reversal. First, at the very moment when we are encouraged to think that Venus' unrelenting assault will be rewarded with success, she is moved by pity for Adonis and resolves "no longer to restrain him" (577). But then, as we anticipate (not for the first time) the imminent departure of Adonis, something arises to delay that leavetaking yet again. With a breathless epizeuxis Venus seeks a meeting for the next day.

> "Tell me, love's master, shall we meet tomorrow?
> Say, shall we, shall we? Wilt thou make the match?"
>   He tells her no, tomorrow he intends
>   To hunt the boar with certain of his friends.
>   (585–88)

The answer of Adonis is cruelly casual. No expression of regret, no suggestion that some other time might be better—only the callous nonchalance with which a social superior announces that he is otherwise engaged and implies a circle from which his interlocutor is excluded. Those who are not in love rarely understand how a casual remark can provoke an earthquake. Adonis' previous reference to the boar (410) had passed unnoticed by Venus, perhaps because it figured as part of a general preference for hunting. Here, however, in the most offhand manner, he announces a meeting with the boar as the direct alternative to a meeting with Venus. The result is a basic change in the situation of the poem. Venus has already argued that procreation is man's only remedy against mortality (169–74), but the truism was too obviously self-interested to carry much weight. Now, however, embodied in the boar, the threat to Adonis' life becomes concrete and immediate. The poem's dominant emotion will veer from comedy to pathos as the opposition between love and hunting emerges as a matter of life and death. The rhetoric of Venus will gain a new intensity as she and we foresee the consequences of its failure.

Botticelli, **Mars and Venus**
(reproduced by courtesy of the Trustees, the National Gallery, London)

Over my altars hath he hung his lance,
His battered shield, his uncontrollèd crest.
(103-04)

Titian, **Venus and Adonis**
(reproduced by permission of the Prado Museum, Madrid)

With this he breaketh from the sweet embrace
Of those fair arms which bound him to her breast.
(811-12)

3

"Danger Deviseth Shifts" Postponing the Boar

If the mention of the boar is a first turning-point in the poem, it is perhaps not surprising that Venus' reaction to it should provide an extreme example of those qualities that have fascinated, perplexed and alienated its readers.

> "The boar!" quoth she, whereat a sudden pale,
> Like lawn being spread upon the blushing rose,
> Usurps her cheek. She trembles at his tale,
> And on his neck her yoking arms she throws.
>   She sinketh down, still hanging on his neck.
>   He on her belly falls, she on her back.
>   (589–94)

We begin with an almost too precious simile that combines half-transparency with the habitual red-white opposition. There is hardly time to appreciate the delicacy of the image before we are stopped short with the slapstick of Venus dragging Adonis down on her belly. Readers like C. S. Lewis object to this kind of thing as undermining the poem's eroticism; others, like Rufus Putney, find confirmation that *Venus and Adonis* should be enjoyed as a rollicking farce. But Shakespeare surely intends us to see that sexual desire, as embodied by

Venus, provides images both of exquisite beauty and of grotesque gymnastics, just as it is composed of acute sensitivity and unthinking aggression. What distinguishes the Shakespeare of *Venus and Adonis* from the Marlowe of *Hero and Leander* and also from Ovid is that, instead of maintaining a fine balance between the extremes, he works with striking juxtapositions and with violent shifts in tone and perspective, obliging us to see love not as a potentially harmonious blend of complementary forces but as an unstable coalition of "variable passions" that is always threatened by division and dissolution.

For a moment Venus seems to have contrived yet another fortunate fall, but this is, in fact, a moment of disintegration. There will be no surfeit of kisses and no culminating image of near-incorporation.

> Now is she in the very lists of love,
> Her champion mounted for the hot encounter.
> All is imaginary she doth prove.
> He will not manage her, although he mount her,
>   That worse than Tantalus is her annoy,
>   To clip Elysium, and to lack her joy.
>   (595–600)

The Tantalus analogy (already suggested at 94) seems almost inevitable for the torture of a separation made more cruel by proximity, but the crucial recognition of the situation comes with "All is imaginary she doth prove." Prince, following Kittredge, takes this as "all that she experiences is mere imagination,"[1] but a better gloss would be "she discovers (proves) that everything is imaginary." What matters is not that we should understand that Venus derives no substantial pleasure, but that Venus herself should be brought to this recognition by the fact that Adonis "will not manage her." The idea of an illusion finally revealed as such is confirmed in the next stanza (601–06) by a recall of

---

[1] Prince, 34.

Pliny's famous story (*Natural History*, 35-36) about the birds deceived by the painted grapes of Zeuxis. However misguided may be the seduction strategies of Venus, what this further development of the feeding metaphor suggests is that the enterprise was doomed from the start, since Adonis is simply not the banquet (445) that Venus imagined him to be. As with the grapes of Zeuxis, there is really nothing to be tasted. And we can accept the implication that Venus, with her truly inventive rhetoric, has been her own Zeuxis.

With the goddess's disappointment likened to that of "poor birds," we have come a long way from the eagle and the vulture. To appreciate the change that has come over Venus we need only look back at previous apparently promising moments. The first kiss (54) had provoked the goddess to a devouring assault (55-60), the second (474) to a bout of orgasmic dying (493-98) and the third (538) to the "desperate courage" of her foraging fury. That erotic aggressivity now evaporates and from this point on she will make no physical attempt to possess Adonis. Even her arguments in favor of procreation will henceforth be governed less by her own appetite than by her need to dissuade Adonis from hunting the boar.

The narrator, who had promised Venus a reward for her persistence (565-76), is now forced to acknowledge, with a wry apostrophe, the failure both of the goddess and of his own prophecy.

> But all in vain, good queen! it will not be.
> She hath assayed as much as may be proved;
> Her pleading hath deserved a greater fee;
> She's Love; she loves; and yet she is not loved.
> (607-10)

The context suggests a play on "assay" as attempt and as the testing of metal. Venus, like a lawyer, has received the fee for her pleading, but on testing the coin of her payment (the "mettle" of Adonis?) she finds that it does not amount to much. The epigrammatic polyptoton of the stanza's fourth line invites comparison with earlier paradoxical summaries of the situation. To be "judge in love" (220) or "queen of love" (251) is not quite the same thing as being Love personified. It is by personifying the passion over which she once held authority that Venus has descended from judge to plaintiff and from queen to subject, discovering in the process a human world where love and power prove incompatible.

Adonis renews his protests with a characteristic reference to his physical discomfort ("you crush me," 611) and Venus replies that her only motive for detaining him is to prevent him from hunting the boar. She begins by dismissing his earlier claim (410) to expertise in the matter.

> "O, be advised; thou know'st not what it is
> With javelin's point a churlish swine to gore,
> Whose tushes, never sheathed, he whetteth still,
> Like to a mortal butcher bent to kill."
> (615–18)

If in the sexual arena Adonis possesses penetrative power without penetrative will, in the hunting field he will have the will without the power. He is mistaken if he believes that in hunting he will be able to display the virility that he has withheld from Venus, for his "javelin's point" will be no match for the murderous tushes of the boar. In a description that owes much to Golding's rendering of Ovid (not the boar that kills Adonis, but the Calydonian boar of *Met*, VIII. 281–97), the emphasis falls heavily on the beast's panoply of penetrative instruments, the "bristly pikes," the snout that "digs sepulchres," the "crooked tushes" (619–24). The boar who is blind to the loveliness of Adonis and who would "root these beauties as he roots the mead" (636) may bear some resemblance to Venus in her more aggressive moods, "devouring all in haste" (57) and foraging with "blindfold fury" (554); but we are surely expected to recognize the difference between an aggressor who seeks to possess beauty and is herself vulnerable and an aggressor who would destroy beauty and who remains himself invulnerable. Shakespeare significantly departs from tradition by omitting any suggestion that Adonis succeeds in wounding the boar.[2] In short, the boar, rather than being a projection of the goddess's own aggressive tendencies, serves to demonstrate how relatively innocuous her aggression really is. We have already seen how the predatory imagery applied to Venus is tempered by more tender moments and redimensioned by revisions (67-72, 559-64); now it is placed in its proper perspective by the introduction of a real predator.

This is not, however, to say that the assault of the boar is entirely unrelated to the passion of Venus. Mention of the boar provokes Venus to a three-stanza excursion (649-66) on jealousy that "doth call himself affection's sentinel," that distempers "gentle love in his desire" and that "eats up love's tender spring." If, on a previous occasion (449) "jealousy" could be glossed as mere apprehension of evil, here the sexual connotations seem unavoidable, especially since jealousy stimulates a prophetic vision of Adonis' death that strongly resembles a rape.

> "And, more than so, presenteth to mine eye
> The picture of an angry chafing boar,
> Under whose sharp fangs on his back doth lie
> An image like thyself, all stained with gore,
>   Whose blood upon the fresh flowers being shed
>   Doth make them droop with grief, and hang the head."
>   (661-66)

A. T. Hatto has argued convincingly that Shakespeare exploits the boar's traditional status as a symbol for destructive lust.[3] Here the

---

[2] In Ovid the boar is pierced with "a glancing blow" (*Met*, X. 712). In Shakespeare Venus tells us that Adonis "ran upon the boar with his sharp spear" (1112), but not that he succeeded in doing any damage. Venus has, in any case, not witnessed the episode she is describing.

[3] A. T. Hatto, "Venus and Adonis—and the Boar," *MLR* 41 (1946), 353-61.

supine position of Adonis, the chafing and the spilling of blood all suggest that Venus has some intuition of the boar as a rival who will deflower Adonis before she does so herself. Since the boar, as Hatto demonstrates, represents not merely lust but its specifically masculine expression, Venus' jealousy and fear are well-founded. Not only does the boar possess the compulsive phallic power that she lacks, but Adonis, "Stain to all nymphs, more lovely than a man" (9), is so constituted as to appeal to male as well as female desire.[4] It would not be surprising if Venus feared some homosexual prevention of her procreative designs. Only in a figurative sense have her own embraces threatened to unman Adonis; now she trembles at the thought of an assault that would more literally cast Adonis in the female role and emasculate the lover she has vainly sought to create.

The balance of the poem has shifted from comedy to pathos, but it is a measure of Shakespeare's tact that the transition is not (and never will be) complete. In the midst of the goddess's anguished foreboding, we are not allowed to forget that this is the same old self-advertising Venus:

> "Didst thou not mark my face? Was it not white?
> Sawest thou not signs of fear lurk in mine eye?
> Grew I not faint, and fell I not downright?
> Within my bosom, whereon thou dost lie,
>   My boding heart pants, beats, and takes no rest,
>   But like an earthquake shakes thee on my breast."
>   (643–48)

Like an actress who is afraid that the audience might miss some of the subtleties of her performance, Venus cannot resist reminding Adonis of how effectively she displays the reactions appropriate to her situation.

---

[4] Lisa Jardine speaks of "a figure vibrant with erotic interest for men." *Still Harping on Daughters: Women and Drama in the Age of Shakespeare* (Brighton, 1993), 18.

In doing so she repeats some of the effects that the narrator has already obtained: "fell I not downright?" ("downe right" in the quarto) has the same kind of ambiguity as "She flatly falleth down" (463) and the hyperbolic earthquake that shakes Adonis on her breast recalls the early vision (31–32) of a hilarious physical disproportion between the protagonists. This is obviously the same Venus who could boast of being supported by primroses (151–52) and then expand her body into a deer-park (229–40), but the undeniably comic effect does not exclude sympathy with her distress. Indeed, it could be argued that Venus is convincing in her anguish precisely because we recognize that she has not been reinvented for the occasion.

The passage on the hunted hare (673–708) takes up a hint in the *Metamorphoses* where Venus dresses like Diana and accompanies Adonis in the hunt—limiting herself, however, to harmless creatures and advising Adonis to do the same:

> hortaturque canes tutaeque animalia praedae,
> aut pronos lepores aut celsum in cornua cervum
> aut agitat dammas; a fortibus abstinet apris
> raptoresque lupos armatosque unguibus ursos
> vitat et armenti saturatos caede leones.
> te quoque, ut hos timeas, siquid prodesse monendo
> posset, Adoni, monet 'fortis'que 'fugacibus esto'
> inquit; 'in audaces non est audacia tuta'.
> (*Met*, X. 537–44)

She also cheers on the hounds and pursues those creatures which are safe to hunt, such as the headlong hares, or the stag with high-branching horns, or the timid doe; but from strong wild boars she keeps away, and from ravenous wolves, and she avoids bears armed with claws and lions reeking with the slaughter of cattle. She warns you too, Adonis, to fear these beasts, if only it were of any avail to warn. 'Be brave against timorous creatures,' she says; 'but against bold creatures boldness itself is not safe.'

Shakespeare's version is enriched with technical details ("doubles," "musits," "cold fault," etc.) of the kind that can be found in manuals like Turbervile's *Booke of Hunting* (1567);[5] but there are surely better reasons for his expansion than the professional pride of a young poet who is eager to show that he has done his homework. Ovid's generic comparison between dangerous predators and "timorous creatures" is little more than a tenuous pretext for the insert-story of Atalanta and Hippomenes (*Met*, X. 560–707) which turns out to be twice as long as the framing story of Venus and Adonis (X. 519–59 and 708–39). Ovid could afford this because his whole poem is one long interweaving of disparate tales. Shakespeare, working in the more restricted form of the epyllion, might want to introduce movement and variety into his rather static poem, but could hardly allow himself to do so with Ovid's sovereign nonchalance. Thus it is that the episode of the hare is made integral to the poem's structure by providing a counterpart to the description of the boar (613–36, 661–66). Unlike Ovid's goddess who simply includes the boar in a list of predators, Shakespeare's Venus has singled out the boar as the embodiment of brute violence and as the real threat to Adonis. She now gives us a corresponding embodiment of animal vulnerability.

If Venus really wants to promote the hunting of the hare, it would seem counter-productive for her to describe the chase in terms that excite so much sympathy for the victim. It becomes, indeed, difficult to dissociate the hare from Adonis who has already been presented as a potential prey, first of Venus and then of the boar, in a world where, as Venus puts it, "misery is trodden on by many, / And, being low, never relieved by any." The couplet—recalling the "relief" once promised by the goddess's landscaped body—gives voice to a compassion that one would not normally associate with the Ovidian gods who, though they may take pity on individual mortals, are hardly distinguished by a

---

[5] See Pooler (1911) cited in Rollins, 68–71.

broad humanitarian outlook. That Venus should express this sense of universal oppression shows how deeply she has become involved in the world. Explicitly she proposes the hare to Adonis as a substitute for the boar; implicitly she is proposing the hare as a substitute for Adonis, a sacrificial offering to the arbitrary violence of nature. Inevitably the hare becomes the focus of her fears and what started out as a strategy to deflect violence away from Adonis only serves to intensify her foreboding. There is a subtle associative shift; the hare now foreshadows not only the fate of Adonis but also the behavior of Venus herself when she follows the hunt in the morning. Just as the hare "cranks and crosses with a thousand doubles" (682), so Venus "treads the path that she untreads again" as her "thousand spleens bear her a thousand ways" (907–08); the hare's "weary legs" are scratched by "each envious brier" (705) and Venus will be impeded by the twining and catching bushes (871–74); the same cry of the hounds that dismays the hare will appall the goddess (882). The resemblances are too striking to be coincidental. In a complex reversal of roles worthy of the *Metamorphoses* (where Actaeon is only the most spectacular example), Venus will hunt Adonis not to make him a prey but to prevent him from becoming one, and in so doing she will behave as if she herself were the prey. In one sense she is already imitating the hare in the act of describing him. Like poor Wat's complex maneuvers, her rhetorical excursions are designed to put off the fatal moment: "Danger deviseth shifts; wit waits on fear" (690).

We are not allowed to dwell on the tragic emotions of terror and pity that Venus may have excited with her representations of predator and prey. The conclusion is a woeful anticlimax:

> "Lie quietly, and hear a little more,
> Nay, do not struggle, for thou shalt not rise.
> To make thee hate the hunting of the boar
> Unlike myself thou hear'st me moralize,

> Applying this to that, and so to so,
> For love can comment upon every woe."
> (709–14)

Bad enough is the reminder that Adonis has been detained more by her physical strength than by the power of her rhetoric; even worse is the fact that the goddess undoes her own good work by, once again, drawing attention to the skill of her performance. Her capacity to "comment upon every woe" is, after all, what prevents Adonis from giving her due attention now when it would finally be in his interest to do so. And, ironically, it is just when the message is so very urgent that Venus fails to conclude her story or draw its moral.

> "Where did I leave?" "No matter where," quoth he;
> "Leave me, and then the story aptly ends.
> The night is spent." "Why what of that?" quoth she.
> "I am," quoth he, "expected of my friends,
>   And now 'tis dark, and going I shall fall."
> "In night," quoth she, "desire sees best of all."
> (715–20)

At the very moment when Venus boasts of her capacity to produce a highly-organized discourse, she loses the thread and lays herself open to a stinging piece of repartee. When she recovers from the interruption, she will revert to earlier arguments in favor of procreation but make no further reference either to the hare or, for that matter, to the boar. There are, in fact, good reasons why Shakespeare may have wanted to interrupt the episode at this point. It could not have been taken much further without arriving at the death of the hare and thus at an intensity of emotion, a premature climax, that would leave little in reserve for later. One may also take the hint that the sacrificial victim has not been accepted; the poem has room for only one death and it will not be that of Wat the hare.

For the second time (see 588) Adonis refers to the companions whom we are never allowed to see. In a situation that offers no other glimpse of a social context Adonis insists that society does exist and that it has claims on him. Implicit are the pride of an adolescent in belonging to an adult male community and the fear that Venus may be a threat to his newly-acquired status. The fragility of that status is neatly captured by his subsequent fear of falling and yet again we wonder how someone so timorous can consider himself qualified to hunt the boar.

Venus embarks on what will be her last speech to Adonis (720–68) and it is a sign of her increasing desperation that now, even more than before, she accumulates hyperboles and conceits in a rapid sequence that threatens to leave the reader behind. Sensing that the end of her speech will mean the departure of Adonis, she is in no mood to worry about logical coherence. Thus, taking up Adonis' fear of falling in the dark, she first seeks to counter it ("In night," quoth she, "desire sees best of all") and then supports it with the suggestion that the earth, in love with Adonis, may trip him up to steal a kiss (721–24). The conceit, however whimsical, is typical of Venus' mindset and anticipates the way she will construe the assault of the boar (1109–18). She cannot bring herself to admit the arbitrary violence of nature: any harm that comes to Adonis must be an accident provoked by the universal desire he awakes. Whether it is the earth who trips Adonis or the boar that gores him, both can be absolved (like Venus herself) on the grounds that they are bewildered by excess of love. As if the earth and the boar were not enough, Venus gives herself another potential rival in Diana, the moon-goddess, who, afraid that Adonis will prove too great a temptation for her chastity, veils herself with clouds "lest she should steal a kiss and die forsworn" (725). The goddess of love may well suspect that Adonis—like her other virginal victim, Hippolytus—is particularly devoted to the goddess of the chase. The conceit amounts to a bitchy hint that Diana's celebrated chastity is in need of some protection and that her patronage of handsome young huntsmen is not entirely above suspicion.[6]

Venus' attack on Diana is another version of the opposition between love and hunting that was announced at the beginning of the poem. In this smear campaign it hardly matters that the accusations are contradictory provided one of them can be made to stick.

> "Now of this dark night I perceive the reason.
> Cynthia, for shame, obscures her silver shine
> Till forging nature be condemned of treason
> For stealing moulds from heaven, that were divine,
>   Wherein she framed thee, in high heaven's despite,
>   To shame the sun by day and her by night."
>   (727–32)

---

[6] The accusation is made explicit in an epigram by Victor Brodeau (1500–40), based on the Latin of the Neapolitan humanist, Girolamo Angeriano (1470–1535):

> Ung jour Venus la belle estoit baisant
> Son Adonis d'affection nayfve.
> Diane alors survint en luy disant,
> "Certes, Venus, tu es par trop lascive
> D'ainsi monstrer ton amour excessive."
> Venus respond: "Tu t'en pourroys bien taire,
> Quant est de moy, je ne crains point de plaire
> A mon amy, des honnestes l'elite.
> Tu fais pis quant en lieu solitaire
> Tu entretiens ne sçay quel Ypolite."

Victor Brodeau, *Poésies*, ed. Hilary M. Tomlinson (Geneva, 1972), 108.

Diana seems to have been widely suspected of hypocrisy. After describing the outraged modesty that provokes her revenge on Actaeon, Fraunce concludes:

> Yet not so austere, yet not so stately Diana,
> But that her owld Mynion with a look more lovely regarding,
> Beautiful Endymion she could finde time to be kissing.
>   (*Yvychurch*, 43)

If Diana (Cynthia) was first seen as enamored of Adonis, now she is pictured as hiding her face through jealousy of his beauty, framed by nature to shame both sun and moon. The "forging nature" that has stolen heavenly moulds recalls "nature that made thee with herself at strife" (11), for in both cases nature is a Promethean artist who exceeds her proper function in creating a perfection reserved for heaven; but whereas, on the previous occasion, nature condemned herself by being left with nothing to strive for, here she risks condemnation from the gods who have been offended by her presumption. Most editors have seen in "forging" and "moulds" a monetary metaphor, but it is surely combined with a sculptural image which is not only fitting for Adonis (213) but also gives to "forging" a creative dignity not present in mere counterfeiting.

Cynthia's reaction to the illegal masterpiece is unworthy of the majesty of outraged law. She resorts to underhand methods in order to thwart the intentions of nature:

> "And therefore hath she bribed the destinies
> To cross the curious workmanship of nature,
> To mingle beauty with infirmities,
> And pure perfection with impure defeature."
> (733–36)

The imagery has shifted from sculpture to tapestry with the weaving "destinies" (Fates) being bribed to create disorder in the web, making a botched job of nature's elaborate design. The dangers that threaten beauty as a result are listed in a catalogue (739–44) that combines mental illness ("frenzies wood," "grief," "damned despair") with a heavy emphasis on physical disease ("fevers," "agues," "pestilence," "surfeits," "impostumes"). The "marrow-eating sickness" is almost certainly syphilis and, as Roe acutely notes, "there would be some irony, and no little guile, in the goddess of *venereal* pursuits blaming any consequent disease on the goddess of chastity."[7] There may also be the broader implication that it is the chastity represented by Diana rather than the excess associated with Venus that has poisoned the source of love: in which case the final curse of Venus (1135-64), which seems to echo this passage, will do little more than spell out the details of a situation created by her rival.

As all these "mad mischances" and assorted maladies "swear nature's death for framing thee so fair" (744), we remember the ambiguity of "the world hath ending with thy life" (12). The real threat, however, is not to the world as such but to the beauty that makes the world worth living in.

> "And not the least of all these maladies
> But in one minute's fight brings beauty under.
> Both favour, savour, hue, and qualities,
> Whereat th'impartial gazer late did wonder,
>   Are on the sudden wasted, thawed, and done,
>   As mountain snow melts with the midday sun."
>   (745-50)

The simile anticipates the moment when Adonis will be "melted like a vapour from her sight" (1166) and also ironically conjures up the coldness that the erotic heat of Venus has been unable to thaw; but for once Venus seems to have risen above the immediate occasion. Purely personal feelings have been submerged in a plangent recognition of the vulnerability and transience of all beauty.

A speech that began merely as a way of detaining Adonis has now gathered genuine momentum and there is no doubting the purposefulness of the rhetoric when Venus concludes with what has always been her strongest argument:

---

[7] Roe, 117.

> "Therefore, despite of fruitless chastity,
> Love-lacking vestals and self-loving nuns,
> That on the earth would breed a scarcity
> And barren dearth of daughters and of sons,
>   Be prodigal. The lamp that burns by night,
>   Dries up his oil to lend the world his light."
>   (751–56)

The idea of procreation as a universal duty allows Venus to present chastity as self-indulgence and sexual intercourse as an act of self-sacrifice; erotic heat is transformed into light. The probable allusion to the parable of the foolish virgins (Matt, 25. 1–3) involves a sacrilegious irony where the wise virgins would be those who do not save the oil and who are, in the application of the metaphor, no longer virgins. Adonis is, in fact, being urged to behave not like the wise virgins but like the prodigal son ("Be prodigal"), and Shakespeare may well be relying on the popular belief that coition involves a loss of vital spirits ("Th'expense of spirit" of Sonnet 129) to underpin the idea that the spending of seminal "oil" is a prodigally generous gesture towards the world.

Two concluding stanzas (757–68) stick with the same chapter of Matthew as we pass from the wise and foolish virgins to the parable of the talents (Matt. 25. 14–30). Adonis, by neglecting the lesson that "gold that's put to use more gold begets," would, like the unprofitable servant, bury his one talent (beauty) together with "that posterity" through which, "by the rights of time," it should be multiplied. "Foul cank'ring rust the hidden treasure frets" echoes the biblical "Lay not up treasures for your selves upon earth, where mothe and canker corrupt" (Matt. 6. 19), but the application is once again ironic in that, far from being enjoined to trust in heaven and eternity, Adonis is being urged to procreate precisely because human time is all that he has. With "in thy pride so fair a hope is slain" (762) the ambiguity of the preposition unites the sense of loss with that of moral condemnation by allowing both positive and negative senses of "pride." The world was entitled to place its hope in the pride of Adonis (prime of life, sexual energy), but that hope has been defeated by his sinful pride (arrogance, self-sufficiency). Though the argument is substantially the same as that of the earlier speech in favor of procreation (163–74), the tone is very different. Venus has moved from relatively bland injunctions—"Thou wast begot, to get it is thy duty" (168), "By law of nature thou art bound to breed" (171)—to a far greater sense of moral outrage:

> "So in thyself thyself art made away,
> A mischief worse than civil, home-bred strife,
> Or theirs whose desperate hands themselves do slay,
> Or butcher sire that reaves his son of life."
> (763–66)

Sexual abstinence has now become worse than civil war, suicide or infanticide. Only the immediate threat of the boar and an increasing sense of desperation can account for this transformation of the goddess who promised uncloying pleasure and unproblematic self-gratification (15–24, 229–40, 397–408) into the sternest of lawgivers.

Venus has stated her strongest argument in the strongest possible terms; it now only needs Adonis to do the same for the situation to reach the breaking-point that has so often seemed imminent and so often been delayed. He rises to the challenge with an unexpected polemical gusto.

> "Nay, then," quoth Adon, "You will fall again
> Into your idle, over-handled theme.
> The kiss I gave you is bestowed in vain,
> And all in vain you strive against the stream;
>   For, by this black-faced night, desire's foul nurse,
>   Your treatise makes me like you worse and worse.
>
> "If love have lent you twenty thousand tongues,
> And every tongue more moving than your own,
> Bewitching like the wanton mermaid's songs,
> Yet from mine ear the tempting tune is blown;

> For know my heart stands armèd in mine ear,
> And will not let a false sound enter there."
>
> (769–80)

He begins with a palpable hit: the one compound adjective "over-handled" suggests that the arguments of Venus are tired clichés, that she is repeating herself and that she is given to hyperbolic excess. If we remember the "wild bird being tamed with too much handling" (560), there is also the hint of an analogy between the way Venus mauls rhetoric and the way she has mauled Adonis who, during his enforced silences, has obviously been gathering ammunition for this speech. The kiss that he has "bestowed in vain" is brought up to reproach Venus as a promise-breaker, and his oath by "this black-faced night, desire's foul nurse" remembers with a negative gloss her claim that by night "desire sees best of all" (720). "Your treatise" harks back to the goddess's boast of her skill in moralizing (712–14) and the "twenty thousand tongues" mocks Venus' own use of numerical hyperbole (516–22). Venus had spoken of the harm inflicted by Adonis' "mermaid voice" (429); he now applies the same image to her in order vaunt his invulnerability. These echoes do more than exemplify the poem's "stylistic principle of antithetical symmetry;"[8] they show that Adonis makes a point of attacking Venus with weapons borrowed from her own armory: anything she says may be taken down and used in evidence against her.

Just as Shakespeare has been careful to maintain a continuity between the old comic Venus and the new pathetic Venus, so he now reminds us that this surprisingly combative Adonis is still, in many respects, a timid adolescent. The proud image of military vigilance evoked by "my heart stands armèd in mine ear" lasts no longer than the break between stanzas:

---

[8] Roe, 118.

> "Lest the deceiving harmony should run
> Into the quiet closure of my breast,
> And then my little heart were quite undone,
> In his bedchamber to be barred of rest.
>   No, lady, no. My heart longs not to groan,
>   But soundly sleeps, while now it sleeps alone."
>   (781–86)

Adonis presumably intends to proclaim the Stoic ideal of a constancy and equanimity undisturbed by desire, but the tone surely betrays a regressive need for infantile security. Adonis seeks to avoid the destiny of the Petrarchan lover whose chamber is transformed from a haven of rest into a place of solitary torment (*O cameretta che già fosti un porto, Canzoniere,* 234), but even more he wants to preserve his bedchamber from an invasion that would make it the site for some activity other than sleeping. Venus may have offered her own body as a protective enclosure (229–40), but this is still dangerously large for the "little heart" of Adonis. The brave sentinel of the previous stanza has been replaced by the antisocial teenager who pleads to be left alone in his room. We need not dwell on the contradiction between this attitude and Adonis' desire to prove himself as a huntsman. Such contradictions are the stuff of adolescence and it is often those who are most timorous and hence least experienced who are likely to run into unconsidered danger.

The relapse is momentary and Adonis soon recovers his argumentative verve.

> "What have you urged that I cannot reprove?
> The path is smooth that leadeth on to danger.
> I hate not love, but your device in love,
> That lends embracements unto every stranger.
>   You do it for increase—O strange excuse,
>   When reason is the bawd to lust's abuse."
>   (787–92)

This would seem to contradict his earlier categorical rejection of love (409–14), but on that occasion he was presumably using the word "love" in the sense just given to it by Venus in her defense of the courser (403–08) and perhaps we should allow for the difference between a situation where he was merely concerned to fend off unwelcome advances and one where he is trying to provide a serious justification of his position. He does not, in fact, deny the doctrine of increase; what he objects to is Venus' use of it as a pretext for promiscuity. The poem may give little evidence for "embracements unto every stranger," but Adonis is generalizing from his own case, the real point being that he is himself a stranger and that Venus has sought carnal knowledge before getting to know him in any other sense.

The climax of the speech (793–804) is like a combination of the ferocious denunciation of lust in Sonnet 129 ("Th'expense of spirit") with the celebration of love in Sonnet 18 ("Shall I compare thee to a summer's day?") As in Sonnet 129, lust is shown as a matter of extremes, beginning as a "hot tyrant" and ending in a premature winter ("Lust's winter comes, ere summer half be done"). The imagery reflects Adonis' own all-too-recent experience: "sweating lust" recalls the sweat of Venus (174) and the "hot tyrant" the generally overheated atmosphere of the encounter. Venus' own feeding imagery ("But O, what banquet wert thou to the taste," 445) is used to counter her argument for increase since lust, like devouring caterpillars, consumes "fresh beauty" and finally "like a glutton dies." Love, by contrast, as in Sonnet 18, is seen as healthily frugal ("Love surfeits not"), essentially temperate ("sunshine after rain," "gentle spring") and immutable ("always fresh"). The catch in all this is that, from the start, Adonis rules out love as an available alternative to lust by situating it in some longlost golden age.

> "Call it not love, for love to heaven is fled
> Since sweating lust on earth usurped his name."
> (793–94)

We remember how Venus also gave her vision of love a prelapsarian flavor ("where never serpent hisses," 17) and how she presented her own body as an Edenic garden (229–40). The debate between Venus and Adonis does not set a down-to-earth realist against a naive idealist. Both protagonists nurture impossible aspirations and neither the initial hedonism of Venus nor the high moral line of Adonis correspond to any reasonable expectations of what love can offer on earth.

The rhetorical technique of Adonis is significantly different from that of Venus—less expansive, less imaginative, but more aphoristic, more pungent. That he should seek to be concise is understandable given the way Venus usually "stops his lips" (46), but there is a significantly tight and buttoned-up quality about his neat antitheses:

> "Love comforteth, like sunshine after rain,
> But lust's effect is tempest after sun.
> Love's gentle spring doth always fresh remain;
> Lust's winter comes ere summer half be done.
>   Love surfeits not; lust like a glutton dies.
>   Love is all truth, lust full of forgèd lies."
>   (799–804)

If this sounds a little too pat to be the fruit of mature reflection, it is to the credit of Adonis that he recognizes the fact:

> "More I could tell, but more I dare not say;
> The text is old, the orator too green."
>   (805–06)

Adonis strengthens his case by forestalling the objections that Venus (and the reader) might feel inclined to make. He sees that his own arguments are no more original than those of Venus and he admits the incongruence between argument and orator. Venus had made a similar admission ("Unlike myself thou hear'st me moralize," 712), but had spoiled the effect by turning it into a boast of her skill (713–14) and carrying on for another eight stanzas (721–68). Adonis knows when to stop and, by ending his speech with the admission that he is an inappropriate speaker, encourages us to consider his argument on its own merits. The "orator too green" has, at least, mastered the essential rhetorical strategy of turning a handicap into an advantage.

And yet Adonis does not depart in triumph. If he has won a rhetorical victory, it obviously does not give him much satisfaction.

> "Therefore in sadness now I will away;
> My face is full of shame, my heart of teen.
> Mine ears that to your wanton talk attended
> Do burn themselves for having so offended."
> (807–10)

Is this a confession that Adonis has, by some culpable passivity, encouraged the advances of Venus? Has he been fascinated, despite his better judgment? Or is it rather that, like many who have been subjected to unwelcome sexual advances, he tends to blame the body for what the mind refuses? After the ringing categorical distinctions of the previous stanzas (793–804), the conclusion is strangely muted. In this debate Adonis was always bound to get the last word if only because the last word is just what Venus' volubility was calculated to avoid. And yet it is an oblique tribute to the rhetoric of Venus that Adonis, who has dismissed it so scornfully, should end by acknowledging its deeply disturbing effect.

4

"With him is Beauty slain"
Death and Metamorphosis

The departure of Adonis is the pivot of the whole poem, the moment when a difficult dialogue is replaced by a desperate monologue and when stalemate gives way to defeat. As Coleridge recognized, the stanza that accomplishes this transition is one of particular brilliance:[1]

> With this he breaketh from the sweet embrace
> Of those fair arms which bound him to her breast,
> And homeward through the dark laund runs apace,
> Leaves love upon her back deeply distressed.
>   Look how a bright star shooteth from the sky,
>   So glides he in the night from Venus' eye.
>
> (811–16)

We are given the scene both as the narrator observes it and as it is experienced by Venus herself. The narrator and Venus share the same

---

[1] "How many images and feelings are here brought together without effort and without discord—the beauty of Adonis—the rapidity of his flight—the yearning yet hopelessness of the enamoured gazer—and a shadowy ideal character is thrown over the whole." Coleridge, *Shakespearean Criticism*, i. 189.

perspective as they watch Adonis hurrying away, but it is the narrator alone who sees in the goddess's position a combination of pathos and physical indignity ("Leaves love upon her back deeply distressed"). The blend of space and obscurity in "dark laund" links the sudden freedom of movement to the threat of imminent extinction while the simile of the shooting star conveys both the elegant motion of Adonis and the specific quality of Venus' attention—not just her wonder at the beauty of Adonis, but also the peculiar kind of intensity needed to grasp and fix a transitory phenomenon. In this context "Look how" is surely more than a synonym for "just as" (compare 67, 289, 925); it becomes like the imperative "look now!" with which one seeks to attract attention to a momentary apparition. Venus, the fixed star, has been transformed into a star-gazer. Finally, "glide" is wonderfully effective because it gives to the ease and rapidity of Adonis' departure a spectral unearthly dimension, contributing to what Coleridge calls "the shadowy ideal character" of the scene. As Adonis moves out of sight, his beauty acquires a magical character which all the eulogies of Venus have failed to convey. The awkward adolescent is transfigured by a brief glory as he glides towards death and towards his definitive mythical status as the embodiment of transient beauty.

The impression of a single action seen from a variety of perspectives is reinforced by the following stanza. Venus follows Adonis with her eye

> Which after him she darts, as one on shore
> Gazing upon a late-embarkèd friend
> Till the wild waves will have him seen no more,
> Whose ridges with the meeting clouds contend.
>   So did the merciless and pitchy night
>   Fold in the object that did feed her sight.
>   (817–22)

The split-second passage of a shooting star might seem incompatible with the gradually diminishing outline of a ship, but the point once again is to underline the quality of Venus' gaze which, precisely because the action is so rapid, seeks to replay it in slow motion as if the pursuing eye could somehow hold Adonis back. The nautical simile paves the way for an image of cosmic disorder as the elements of water and air mingle on a stormy horizon; the darkness, which might first have seemed a backdrop to enhance the brightness of starlike Adonis, now becomes an active threatening force which reaches out to "fold" him in an embrace more deadly than that of the enfolding arms from which he has escaped. A similar combination of elements makes Venus herself the victim both of the water which has swallowed her "precious jewel" (824) and of the darkness in which she has "lost the fair discovery of her way" (828). The phrase reflects ironically on her claim that by night "desire sees best of all" (720) and, if she now remains immobile ("confounded in the dark she lay," 827), it is simply because she has nowhere to go: the darkened path leads not to Adonis but only into the darkness that has swallowed him.

The loquacity of Venus is not checked by the disappearance of Adonis, but Shakespeare's decision to rely on reported speech at this point is important, if only because the situation of the abandoned or betrayed woman is traditionally one that, from Ovid's *Heroides* on, invites the male author to impersonate a female voice. The really interesting thing about the Female Complaint is that, given its monologic amplitude, the genre's "repeatedly male structuring of the feminine"[2] involves a whole series of assumptions about the woman's use of rhetoric. Since the formal study of rhetoric was seen as a preparation for that public life from which women were excluded, the problem facing the male poet was how to create a genuinely expressive female voice without granting women the rhetorical competence reserved for men. The tradition of the Female Complaint provided its own solution by depriving rhetoric of its primary function as

---

[2] John Kerrigan, *Motives of Woe: Shakespeare and "Female Complaint": A Critical Anthology* (Oxford, 1991), 8.

persuasion. The framing narrator (almost always envisaged as male) is rarely much more than an eavesdropper and the woman usually speaks in a situation without hope and without a real addressee. In such a context the *copia* and ingenuity that would signal rhetorical competence in a male speaker risk appearing as fruitless repetition or sheer female garrulousness, as they tend to do in *Lucrece*. Of all the Renaissance genres none seems more expressly designed to let the poet indulge his sympathy for the female condition while simultaneously confirming the period's stereotypes of female inferiority.

Shakespeare, however, has already given Venus the purposeful rhetoric, the discourse of desire rather than loss, that is usually reserved for the male. After such a switch in gender roles, the Venus who reverts to the tradition of the Female Complaint is, he implies, simply not worth hearing. The reader need not be given the actual words of Venus because the whole exercise is entirely predictable. It is enough that we be reminded of what the genre demands—"a wailing note," "a woeful ditty" (835–36), relying on the most conventional forms of paradox and antithesis ("How love is wise in folly, foolish-witty," 838), tedious, self-indulgent, and potentially endless:

> Her song was tedious, and outwore the night;
> For lovers' hours are long, though seeming short.
> If pleased themselves, others, they think, delight
> In such-like circumstance, with such-like sport.
>   Their copious stories oftentimes begun
>   End without audience and are never done.
>   (841–46)

Shakespeare's parodistic approach to a genre that purports to represent the spontaneous effusion of sentiment while remaining tied to literary convention is made clear when the ditty that Venus is supposed to sing "extemporally" is, immediately after, presented in terms that suggest the fixed procedure of a liturgy:

> Her heavy anthem still concludes in woe,
> And still the choir of echoes answer so.
> (839–40)

Parody apart, the echo, a common feature of solitary laments, serves a double function. On the one hand, it amplifies the expression of emotion ("Passion on passion deeply is redoubled," 832) until it fills the whole landscape ("all the neighbour caves," 830); on the other hand, simply because it fills all the available space with the one human voice, it reminds us that the pathetic fallacy is indeed a fallacy. Echoes are not answers and, if we try to imagine them as such, they will turn out to be unsympathetic:

> For who hath she to spend the night withal
> But idle sounds resembling parasites,
> Like shrill-tongued tapsters answering every call,
> Soothing the humour of fantastic wits?
> (847–50)

With this final touch of derision, the goddess of love, unable to find a companion for the night, is reduced to the level of those poor relicts who seek relief from solitude in the fake fellowship of the tavern.

By treating the complaint in this manner Shakespeare provides a welcome break from the direct speech of the goddess that has been dominant so far; he also confirms the pattern already noted (643–48, 709–14) of restoring an ironic distance at the very moment when pathos threatens to take over. More daringly, by evoking what the Female Complaint has to offer at its familiar worst, Shakespeare draws our attention to the virtuosity of his own performance when he decides to take the genre seriously in the closing Lament of Venus (1069–1188). There is nothing unusual about an author parodying his past successes, but only a poet almost insolently sure of his means could take the risk of using a parody to anticipate the real thing.

Venus' nocturnal complaint is cut short by an aubade, the song of the lark that heralds the second sunrise in the poem:[3]

> Lo, here the gentle lark, weary of rest,
> From his moist cabinet mounts up on high
> And wakes the morning, from whose silver breast
> The sun ariseth in his majesty,
>   Who doth the world so gloriously behold
>   That cedar tops and hills seem burnished gold.
>   (853–58)

The stanza's efficacy derives from an elaborate sequence of contrasts—between the lark, "weary of rest," and Venus who has passed a night without rest, between the freshness of "his moist cabinet" and the thick taproom atmosphere of the previous stanza, between the invigorating song that "wakes the morning" and the "tedious" song that "outwore the night," between the flight of the bird and the heavy earthbound situation of the goddess. Inevitably, we compare this sunrise with the one that opened the poem: in both we have the metaphor of the sun as lover leaving the bed of his mistress, the morning. But Roe is wide of the mark when he speaks of the more measured and dignified manner of the second sunrise as "anticipating the solemnity of the events which will follow."[4] The earlier sunrise, with its imagery of separation and tearfulness, obviously did foreshadow the day's events. Not so this sunrise where the exhilaration of the lark and the golden glory of the landscape give no hint of the impending catastrophe. Here, at least, nature resembles its representation (the "painted grapes" of 601–06) in that its promises prove equally unreliable.

---

[3] Many critics have followed Coleridge in citing this stanza as one of the poem's local felicities. Sir Henry Rowley Bishop's 1819 setting for soprano and flute remained a popular recital piece well into the twentieth century.

[4] Roe, 122.

Venus responds to the sunrise with what sounds at first like the opening of a Neoplatonic hymn celebrating the source of universal light:

> "O thou clear god, and patron of all light,
> From whom each lamp and shining star doth borrow
> The beauteous influence that makes him bright."
> (860–62)

This is the tone of Spenser's *Fowre Hymns* and we might expect the invocation to conclude with a prayer for the safety of Adonis. Venus, however, has already said that the brightness of Adonis is framed "to shame the sun by day" (732) and now she profits from the inescapable pun to push the hyperbole to a point where it would seem to invite retaliation:

> "There lives a son that sucked an earthly mother
> May lend thee light as thou dost lend to other."
> (863–64)

If, in many readings of the myth, Adonis is indeed identified with the sun, here any such allusion can only be ironic. The Adonis of the poem is all too human, all too mortal, and not even the rhetoric of a goddess will succeed in giving him cosmic status. Jonathan Bate sees a further irony in the fact that Adonis, born from a tree, never has "sucked an earthly mother;"[5] but whether Venus has forgotten this or not is less important than our recognition that, in her protective and nutritive aspect (229–40, 875–76), the goddess tries and fails to become a surrogate human mother.

The poem breaks into movement as Venus "hasteth to a myrtle grove" (865), presumably hoping to renew her wooing of Adonis in the

---

[5] Bate, 55.

more auspicious setting provided by her favorite tree (an improvement on the "ragged bough," 37). Hearing the hounds and horn, she changes direction and "coasteth to the cry" (870), guided to Adonis only by sound, just as his hounds are guided to the boar only by scent. This generalized and confused movement, involving all three protagonists, stands in marked contrast to the static deadlocked struggle of the first section.

The running of Venus contains an ironic echo of Daphne's flight from Apollo where the vegetation impedes the one who is seeking to evade love (*Met*, I. 508–09); but here the goddess has none of the elegance that we associate with Ovid's fleet-footed heroines. What she had imagined for Adonis—the earth tripping him to steal a kiss (721–23)—becomes almost true of herself:

> And as she runs, the bushes in the way
> Some catch her by the neck, some kiss her face,
> Some twine about her thigh to make her stay.
> She wildly breaketh from their sweet embrace,
>   Like a milch doe whose swelling dugs do ache,
>   Hasting to feed her fawn hid in some brake.
>   (871–76)

The echo of "With this he breaketh from the sweet embrace" (811) is too obvious to be coincidental: the amorous bushes seek to entangle Venus much as she entangled Adonis. This, we remember, is the goddess who could "Dance on the sands, and yet no footing seen" (148) and who has argued for the lightness of love (150). In the event, as we have seen from her repeated fallings (463, 546, 594), love turns out to be like the force of gravity dragging her down to a literally earthbound condition. The comparison with the "milch doe" once again underlines the indignity and the pathos of that descent. For a moment only we may be iconoclastically tempted to think of the legendary breasts of Venus as "swelling dugs;" the suckling imagery (see 863) surely invites sympathy for the goddess's frustrated maternal instinct. How does this reflect on Adonis' claim that Venus' arguments in favor of procreation are merely a "strange excuse" for lust (791)? What is strange, in the sense of confounding expectations, is that Venus should see Adonis both as a child and as potential father of her child. Bate, arguing for the "contextual pressure" exerted on *Venus and Adonis* by Ovid's Myrrha story, sees the implication that "Adonis is forced to re-enact, with gender and generational roles reversed, his mother's incestuous affair."[6] This, however, is to mistake the half-conscious inclinations of Venus for what actually happens in the poem where Adonis, after all, succeeds in his resistance. It would, if anything, be more plausible to find in the fate of Myrrha an explanation of why Adonis can *not* be forced into a relation that smacks of incest. And perhaps we do not really need the Myrrha story as "an ironic, darkening pre-text"[7] to see how the figure of Venus embodies not only male fantasies of desire but also male fears of the confusing and threatening aspects of female sexuality.

Venus hears that the hounds are "at a bay" (877) and concludes that this is not the "gentle chase" she had recommended but the "blunt boar, rough bear, or lion proud" (884). Her fear propels her from one extreme to the other, from violent motion to a trembling standstill and from an extraordinary acuteness of the senses to a paralysis that "numbs each feeling part" (892). And it is precisely when she begins to recover that, with a sudden change from the uncertain indications of hearing to the incontrovertible evidence of sight, she spies "the hunted boar" (900). Venus has, in anticipation, already given an itemized description of the boar—his tushes, back, bristles, snout, sides, neck (613–30): when she actually sees him, he is reduced to a mouth, "a frothy mouth, bepainted all with red, / Like milk and blood being mingled both together." The red and white, first introduced to suggest harmonious beauty (10) and then developed as the misleading manifestations of conflicting emotions (35–36, 76, 345–48, 467–68),

---

[6] Bate, 54.
[7] Bate, 55.

now provide an image of startling perversity—especially if we remember the tempting red mouth of Adonis (451–56) and the breastfeeding associated with Venus. The whole image seems to be a nightmarish transposition of Venus' maternal and sexual instincts.

Once again Venus breaks into movement, but this time without any sense of direction:

> A thousand spleens bear her a thousand ways.
> She treads the path that she untreads again.
> Her more than haste is mated with delays,
> Like the proceedings of a drunken brain,
>   Full of respects, yet naught at all respecting;
>   In hand with all things, naught at all effecting.
>   (907–12)

Here the proliferation of rhetorical figures (ploke, antithesis, polyptoton) is calculated to create confusion rather than order. The couplet might almost be taken as a reflection on her attitude throughout the poem. The goddess who both defies and recommends conventional gender roles, who is attracted to a male by his female appearance and who sees in Adonis both child and potential husband, is truly "in hand with all things, naught at all effecting," doomed to failure by the sheer range and incompatibility of her desires.

The chorus of howling with which the hounds of Adonis answer the desperate inquiries of Venus (918–24) recalls the derisive echoes awakened by her nocturnal complaint (829–52). The voices of nature can only confirm her misery or mock her with their stubborn incomprehensibility. There is no need here for talking animals; one look at their dejected demeanor is enough for Venus to imagine the worst:

> Look how the world's poor people are amazed
> At apparitions, signs, and prodigies,
> Whereon with fearful eyes they long have gazed,
> Infusing them with dreadful prophecies:

> So she at these sad signs draws up her breath,
> And, sighing it again, exclaims on death.
> (925–30)

We may take "poor" not only as an expression of sympathy for all those who believe in omens, but also as an indication of social status: if we read the object of "infusing" as the "signs, and prodigies" then the sense would be that Venus, like the poor who always have reason to expect the worst, endows any unusual natural phenomenon with ominous significance. The heavenly queen has been reduced to the rank of a superstitiously fearful plebeian—the irony being that, in this case, the fear turns out to be perfectly justified.

Venus launches into a four-stanza chiding of death (931–54), complete with all the appropriate rhetorical figures: systrophe ("hard-favoured tyrant," "divorce of love," "earth's worm"), epiplexis ("what dost thou mean?"), aposiopesis and correctio ("If he be dead—O no, it cannot be . . . O yes, it may"). The "grim-grinning ghost" (presumably a skull) and the worm are familiar features of charnel-house imagery linked by the idea of blindness and preparing us for the conceit that Adonis is slain only because death has "no eyes to see" (939). The passage is dense with recollections and anticipations. Since Elizabethan usage allowed "worm" as a synonym for "snake," we may think of death as the serpent from whom the goddess had promised protection in her embrace (17). At the same time, when she complains that death, instead of cropping a weed, has plucked a flower (946), we remember her own argument that flowers should be "gathered in their prime" (131) and think forward to her final gesture after the metamorphosis (1175). Typical of Venus is the strong suggestion that the tragedy results from some ghastly misunderstanding of instructions—flower instead of weed, "death's ebon dart" instead of "Love's golden arrow"

(947–48).[8] It is all in keeping with her final exoneration of the boar who will be reproached for inadvertency rather than malevolence.

The final couplet of the speech is given epigrammatic force by the oxymoron of "mortal vigour" and by the ambiguity of "rigour" (lack of pity and *rigor mortis*):

> "Now nature cares not for thy mortal vigour,
> Since her best work is ruined with thy rigour."
> (953–54)

We recall "nature with herself at strife" (11). Nature, having created the ideal form in Adonis, was left with nothing to aim at. Now death is in a similar position since he has completed his negative masterpiece in the destruction of that perfection. Nature has nothing more to fear because death has nothing more to achieve, and Venus no longer sees the death of Adonis as the end of the world, but rather as the end of meaning, since both nature and death are left without a purpose.

Faithful to his practice of arousing and withdrawing from pathos, Shakespeare again takes his distance from Venus—this time not an ironic but an aesthetic distance. In the midst of her grief, Venus retains or regains the beauty that we expect of her: the "crystal tide" of tears flowing in "the sweet channel of her bosom" (957–58) helps to repair any damage that might have been done by "swelling dugs" (875), and the shift is reinforced by the development given to "crystal":

> O how her eyes and tears did lend and borrow!
> Her eye seen in her tears, tears in her eye,
> Both crystals, where they viewed each other's sorrow.
> (961–63)

---

[8] Malone mentions Whitney's *Choice of Emblemes* (1586) where we find the story of Love and Death exchanging arrows by mistake. Cited by Roe, 126.

Wyndham saw an allusion to the magic crystals of Dr. Dee "in which one in sympathy with another could see the scene of his distress;"[9] but this is less immediately striking than the image of a crystal seen in a crystal which combines the Shakespearean feeling for translucence with a foreboding of the double vision that will follow Venus' discovery of the body of Adonis (1063–68). For a moment Venus, like the Cordelia who is "sunshine and rain at once" (*Lear* Q, xvii. 19), embodies the strange harmony that can be wrought out of contrasting emotions:

> Variable passions throng her constant woe,
> As striving who should best become her grief.
> All entertained, each passion labours so
> That every present sorrow seemeth chief,
>   But none is best. Then join they all together,
>   Like many clouds consulting for foul weather.
>   (967–72)

Yet "best become" is, after all, ambiguous: the "variable passions" strive to see which of them can make her grief most beautiful, but they also compete to become the major cause of that grief and end by conspiring to produce a day not of changing loveliness but of unremitting "foul weather."

Venus hears "some huntsman hollo" (973) and imagines it to be the voice of Adonis. Seizing on the slightest evidence, her "variable passions" provoke a series of reversals. The sounds of the hunt had been the cause of her fear; now they become the grounds of her hope: where Venus had been the nursing mother and Adonis the child, now momentarily Venus seems the child and Adonis the nurse ("A nurse's song ne'er pleased her babe so well," 974). The tears that had fallen so profusely now "turn their tide" and remain "prisoned in her eye like

---

[9] Wyndham, 221.

pearls in glass" (979–80) or, if they fall, are melted by her cheek which will not permit them

> To wash the foul face of the sluttish ground,
> Who is but drunken when she seemeth drowned.
> (983–84)

We are clearly being moved away from the Venus who, at the start of the poem, seemed an embodiment of lust and also from the maudlin tavern bore of the nocturnal lament (847–52). Now it is the ground that is "sluttish" and "drunken," unworthy to be washed by tears that have touched the cheek of a goddess.

Venus, however, is not yet fully restored to her Olympian status. The emphasis still falls on her febrile instability:

> O hard-believing love—how strange it seems
> Not to believe, and yet too credulous!
> Thy weal and woe are both of them extremes.
> Despair, and hope, makes thee ridiculous.
> The one doth flatter thee in thoughts unlikely;
> In likely thoughts the other kills thee quickly.
> (985–90)

Once again we have a complex pattern of antithesis which, like the antimetabole that so often accompanies it, is a dominant figure in this poem of systematic oppositions and reversals. Love is, of course, both Venus herself at this moment and love in general which is characterized by contradictions and "extremes." "Hard-believing" is deliberately and radically ambiguous since it can be construed as "holding a firm belief" and "finding it hard to believe." Both senses are borne out by what follows. Venus goes from the extreme of despair to the extreme of hope and both make her "ridiculous." We should not be misled by the adjective: the extremes of Venus, frequently comic when she was trying to seduce Adonis, can now be a source of ridicule only to an observer who does not know her all-too-real grounds for anxiety, and the narrator has made sure that the reader is in no such position.

Flattered by hope, Venus turns to flatter death in a speech so groveling that it reveals just how fragile her hope really is. With a strategy not very different from that implicit in her account of the hunted hare (673–708), she attempts to break the alliance between death and the boar by proposing the boar as a victim in place of Adonis.

> "'Tis not my fault; the boar provoked my tongue.
> Be wreaked on him, invisible commander.
> 'Tis he, foul creature, that hath done thee wrong.
> I did but act; he's author of thy slander.
>   Grief hath two tongues, and never woman yet
>   Could rule them both, without ten women's wit."
> (1003–08)

The irony here is that the boar could plead the same excuse as Venus. Venus argues that she has been merely the actor in a script whose author is the boar. But the boar might claim that he is no more than the material agent of a crime whose true author is Death. The metaphor is theatrical as well as legal: Shakespeare, as both author and actor, would know how difficult it can be to apportion responsibility.

There is not much dignity left in a goddess who pleads that, as a mere woman, she cannot be expected to govern her tongue; but the really abject self-abasement is that of an immortal who seeks to propitiate the very power that we would assume she need not fear. The climax of her speech is, in fact, an implicit recognition of her limits. Immortal herself, she cannot confer immortality upon Adonis and that is why she tries so hard to convince herself that he must, at least, have the same permanence as the cosmic order.

> "O Jove," quoth she, "how much a fool was I
> To be of such a weak and silly mind

> To wail his death who lives, and must not die
> Till mutual overthrow of mortal kind!
> For he being dead, with him is beauty slain,
> And beauty dead, black chaos comes again."
> (1015–20)

Shakespeare may be remembering the description of chaos that opens the *Metamorphoses* (I. 5–20) and there is more than a hint of the Neoplatonic concept of pure forms emerging from the primeval chaos that would return if they were destroyed. Such resonances do not, however, make *Venus and Adonis* anything like a Neoplatonic poem. For Venus Neoplatonism is no more than a straw at which she grasps in her search for reassurance. The reader, here as elsewhere (11–12, 729–30, 863–64, 953–54) remains conscious of the exasperated hyperbole that transforms a handsome boy into a guarantee of the cosmic order. *Venus and Adonis* as a whole always manages to defeat the Neoplatonic readings that its details sometimes seem to invite.

Already Venus seems to have forgotten that her speech began as an address to death. What matters now is that her fears should be proved irrational both from a theoretical standpoint, as inconsistent with cosmic order, and in the light of direct sense experience as "trifles unwitnessèd with eye or ear" (1023). One thinks of the expression "eyewitness" as particularly relevant to a poem that repeatedly urges the reader to "see" or "look" and in which mention of the "eye" so often involves an almost painful sense of its physical reality as a bodily organ. Venus, happily deceived by the witness of the ear, is about to learn the very different effect of witnessing on the eye.

> As falcons to the lure, away she flies,
> The grass stoops not, she treads on it so light;
> And in her haste unfortunately spies
> The foul boar's conquest on her fair delight.
> (1027–30)

There is a clear reminiscence of her boasted lightness (145–56), but the simile of the falcon and the lure both recalls her earlier role as sexual predator (eagle, 55–60, and vulture, 547–52) and anticipates her final disappointment. When we finally reach the catastrophe that has been so often anticipated, the effect is surprisingly muted. Even if we allow for "unfortunately" having "a stronger sense than modern usage,"[10] the lines still sound almost like a euphemism for what has actually occurred. Ovid, for all his brevity, still finds time for "the groans of the dying youth" which Venus hears from afar before she sees him "lying lifeless and weltering in his blood" (*Met*, X. 719–21), and Renaissance versions of the story do not usually spare the gory details. One might say that Shakespeare avoids the kind of physical details that would evoke horror rather than pathos, but such aesthetic caution would hardly be consistent with his practice elsewhere in the poem. What the lines do convey is the sense of a sight so unexpected that its details cannot be immediately grasped. In this context the verb "spies" is more than a synonym for "sees." It has already been used, within a similar structure, for Venus' sight of the boar ("And with that word she spied the hunted boar," 900). In both cases it suggests something that impinges suddenly and obliquely on an eye that is unprepared for what it sees.

The sight of the frothy-mouthed boar (901–06) had roused Venus from a paralysis of the senses into frantic movement. With the sight of Adonis the process is reversed: her chase comes to a sudden halt and she loses the sense of sight.

> Which seen, her eyes, as murdered with the view,
> Like stars ashamed of day, themselves withdrew.
> (1031–32)

---

[10] Evans, 204.

Adonis has, of course, already been associated with the sun (198, 732, 863–64) and it is conventional enough to say that, when day comes, the stars withdraw because they are put to shame by the sun's superior brightness; but here the simile is given an unexpected twist. The stars withdraw not because of the sun's brilliance but because that brilliance has been extinguished in death. There is more than a hint of survivor's guilt: since the stars would be unable to shine by day if the sun were alive, they feel ashamed of doing so now that he lies slain. The simile is, perhaps, over-condensed and confused by the fact that the eyes are seen first as "murdered" and then as "ashamed;" but "murdered" may just possibly have the sense of "damaged" or "bruised" as in the French *meurtri*. This would provide a bridge to the subsequent extended simile of the snail.

> Or as the snail, whose tender horns being hit
> Shrinks backward in his shelly cave with pain,
> And there, all smothered up, in shade doth sit,
> Long after fearing to creep forth again;
>   So at his bloody view her eyes are fled
>   Into the deep dark cabins of her head.
>   (1033–38)

The snail, like the divedapper, the lark and the hunted hare, has often been cited as evidence of Shakespeare's instinctive sympathy with animals or of his fresh "unliterary" natural observation. Keats, who first attributes the simile to "one of these sonnets" and then proceeds to confuse it with a similar passage on the "cockled snails" in *Love's Labours Lost*, is only one of a long line of nineteenth-century critics who made a habit of celebrating such passages in isolation from their context.[11] The truth is, however, that the passage derives its power not only from its naturalistic accuracy or from the startling association of a

---

[11] *The Letters of John Keats 1814–21*, 2 vols., ed. H. E. Rollins (Cambridge, Mass., 1958), I, 189.

goddess with a small and despised animal, but from the place it occupies in a whole network of images that link the "variable passions" of Venus to the animal world. Implicitly or explicitly she has been seen as sharing the destructive rapacity of the eagle and the vulture, the instinctive sexuality of the horses, the fear of the hunted hare, the maternal anxiety of the milch doe and the credulity of the lured falcon. Now, at one extreme end of the scale in terms of size, vulnerability and sensitivity comes the snail. Venus, who had presented her own body as an alternative landscape, free from the habitual insecurity and instability of the natural world, has become herself so enmeshed in that world that she experiences the whole range of its multiple manifestations and contradictory compulsions. There is rather more to the oft-proclaimed earthiness of Venus than a strong sexual appetite.[12]

The two following stanzas (1039–50) seek to explain Venus' reaction in terms of an elaborate but conventional analogy between the physical body and the body politic, with the eyes as state officials, the brain as chief counselor and the heart as king. It is, no doubt, the kind of passage that Hazlitt had in mind when he remarked that, in the narrative poems, "a beautiful thought is sure to be lost in an endless commentary upon it."[13] Shakespeare exploits the same analogy to better effect elsewhere (*Caesar*, II. i. 66–69); here it only serves to dissipate the painful immediacy of the snail image.

What Venus sees when she reopens her eyes is the juxtaposition of red and white that has pervaded the whole poem:

> And, being opened, threw unwilling light
> Upon the wide wound that the boar had trenched
> In his soft flank, whose wonted lily-white

---

[12] For a stimulating though not entirely sympathetic discussion of how the snail simile functions, see W. B. C. Watkins, *Shakespeare and Spenser* (Princeton, NJ, 1950), 3–24.

[13] Hazlitt, 265.

150 VARIABLE PASSIONS

> With purple tears that his wound wept was drenched.
> No flower was nigh, no grass, herb, leaf, or weed,
> But stole his blood, and seemed with him to bleed.
> (1051–56)

If "trenched" suggests the brutal rooting-up of beauty that Venus had foreseen (635–36), the "wonted lily-white" drenched with "purple tears" recalls the colors that gave Adonis his beauty in life, thus transforming the incipient horror into aesthetic pathos. Venus had already claimed that the "breath and beauty" of Adonis conferred "gloss on the rose, smell to the violet" (935–36); it is, therefore, predictable that the whole of nature should suffer from his loss. And yet the phrasing is ambiguous. The plants seem to bleed and hence to die with Adonis, but they also steal his blood as if it held the secret of their own renewal. This would be perfectly consistent with the view of Adonis as a vegetative god whose death both brings winter and ensures continued fertility. As always, however, this mythological reading is no more than faintly invited. The whole image, indeed, is presented with a non-committal "seemed" and it is only Venus ("This solemn sympathy poor Venus noteth," 1057) who takes the pathetic fallacy for a fact.

Deprived of speech, Venus is reduced to mimic gestures like an actor in a dumb-show ("Dumbly she passions," 1059) and even over these gestures she loses control ("her joints forget to bow," 1061). We are surely intended to remember the splendid performance of passion with which Venus anticipated this event and which she invited Adonis to admire (643–48). Having mourned so much in advance, she is now furious at the thought that she may have nothing left in reserve for the real thing. "Her eyes are mad that they have wept till now" (1062), and the ambiguity of "mad" (angry and insane) leads on to the mental disorder that provokes a disturbance of vision (1063–68). The eyes that had first refused to see now see too much. The very intensity of her gaze "makes the wound seem three" while "his face seems twain; each several limb is doubled." There have been so many images of doubleness in the poem—the eyes reflected in eyes (119–20), Narcissus and his shadow in the brook (161–62), the white of alabaster enclosing the white of ivory (361–64), the two crystals of eyes and tears (961–63)—that this appears as the culmination of a conscious design. *Venus and Adonis* is a poem which achieves some of its most characteristic effects by blurring and reflection, by troubling the boundaries between reality and representation, self and Other. The narrator comments knowingly that "oft the eye mistakes, the brain being troubled," and the tone, if one may allow the anachronism, is that of a sixteenth-century neurologist, a colleague of the physician in *Macbeth*, dispassionate though not unsympathetic, faced by a condition where he can offer a diagnosis but no cure.

The double vision stimulates Venus to a bitter conceit:

> "My tongue cannot express my grief for one,
> And yet," quoth she, "behold two Adons dead!"
> (1069–70)

We know that this kind of adynaton—pleading the inadequacy of words or the incompetence of the speaker—is often the prelude to a virtuoso display of eloquence, and so it is in this case. The pithiness of the conceit is the first sign of Venus' recovery. From now to the end of the poem we shall see how she uses her formidable rhetorical powers (as she did with the Mars-Venus episode, 97–114) to reshape the whole story in a way that satisfies her self-esteem. This is not to say that her grief is somehow insincere, but that, having lost her divine prerogatives by descending to human love, she gains the human privilege of using language to give unacceptable experience an acceptable aesthetic form.

Venus explains her lack of sighs and tears by what has happened to their sources in the heart and the eyes:

> "My sighs are blown away, my salt tears gone,
> Mine eyes are turned to fire, my heart to lead.

> Heavy heart's lead melt at mine eyes' red fire!
> So shall I die by drops of hot desire."
> (1071–74)

The goddess, whose sighs and tears have failed to melt the heart of Adonis, now urges her own heart to melt; but the image, framed by the emphatic figures of antimetabole and anadiplosis, has none of the tenderness and emotional release that we usually associate with the melting heart. On the contrary, it recalls the atrocious suffering of someone being slowly tortured to death by drops of molten lead (wonderfully conveyed by the accumulation of accented monosyllables in 1073). At the same time, dying "by drops of hot desire" suggests that she hopes to find in death the orgasm that Adonis failed to provide. The irony is that Venus, as an immortal, is no more capable of dying than she was of seducing Adonis. The image is so violent and peremptory precisely because she is asking for the impossible.

Reverting to the "solemn sympathy" (1057) between Adonis and nature, Venus commiserates with the world which is left without any beauty to boast of:

> "Alas, poor world, what treasure hast thou lost,
> What face remains alive that's worth the viewing?
> Whose tongue is music now? What canst thou boast
> Of things long since, or anything ensuing?
>   The flowers are sweet, their colours fresh and trim;
>   But true sweet beauty lived and died with him."
> (1075–80)

The stanza is of a piece with her insistence on Adonis as the only source and guarantee of beauty in the world (935–36) and with her prophecies about the cosmic catastrophe that waits upon his death—the world that will end with his life (12), the "mutual overthrow of mortal kind" (1018) and the return of "black chaos" (1020). The couplet, however, makes it clear that this is now only a last despairing attempt to deny the evidence of nature's indifference. What Venus, like many a survivor, cannot admit is that the world should continue in its old unfeeling course. Thus her attitude will fluctuate between commiseration and blame: nature may have loved Adonis or it may have conspired to destroy him, but she cannot imagine that it has been simply unconcerned.

Since "true sweet beauty" no longer exists, there is no longer any need for bonnet or veil as a protection against the rough embrace of sun or wind which had "lurked like two thieves" to rob Adonis of his beauty (1081-86). The paronomasia in "Having no fair to lose, you need not fear" links beauty to anxiety and relies on the conceit of beauty as a commodity (treasure) that cannot be simultaneously kept by its owner and *possessed* by someone else. A similar logic is present in all the images of Venus as predator, hunter or feeder and of Adonis as prey, cropped fruit or plucked flower. Venus herself has urged that beauty must yield to possession in order to perpetuate itself through offspring (169-74, 757-68), but her argument is undermined by the fact that elsewhere she sees Adonis not as a steward of beauty (like the fair youth of the matrimonial sonnets) but as beauty itself which must, therefore, die with him (11-12) whether he procreates or not. It follows that she can never be sure whether to regard the natural cycle as an ally or as an enemy. Here nature reflects Venus' own combination of desire (striving to kiss Adonis) and aggression (seeking to steal his beauty), but it is significant for her rewriting of experience that she soon softens the image into one of playful complicity:

> "And therefore would he put his bonnet on,
> Under whose brim the gaudy sun would peep.
> The wind would blow it off, and, being gone,
> Play with his locks; then would Adonis weep.
>   And straight, in pity of his tender years,
>   They both would strive who first should dry his tears."
> (1087-92)

154 VARIABLE PASSIONS

We remember the youth's fear of sunburn (186) and Venus herself lifting his bonnet (351).[14] She had once accused him of narcissism (157–62), but now she regards that same characteristic with nostalgic tenderness. It need hardly be said that this pretty child who weeps for the loss of his bonnet is a travesty of the Adonis we have seen in the poem. Venus is already transforming the story in a way that eliminates all the asperities of her desire and his determined resistance. The result is her Edenic picture of a natural world that derived harmony from his presence (1093–104). Not only did the lion and wolf refrain from attacking him, the birds bring him fruit and the fishes gild his shadow in the brook, but the routine violence between creatures was suspended:

> "If he had spoke, the wolf would leave his prey,
> And never fright the silly lamb that day."
> (1097–98)

There are memories here of the beast-taming Orpheus and perhaps even of the marvelous child in Isaiah (xi. 6) and in Virgil's Fourth Eclogue. Adonis presides, like a beneficent god, over an unfallen world where all the creatures bask in his life-giving regard. It is a remarkable transformation of the poem's unidyllic setting which, as we have seen, is replete with suffering and slaughter. Venus seems to have forgotten that Adonis himself was a hunter, and yet it may be doubted whether the poem invites us to reproach her for this self-indulgent distortion of the facts. As with Cleopatra's celebration of Antony (*Antony*, V. ii. 76–99), there is an undeniable grandeur in the spirit that can create a

---

[14] For the sixteenth century there was nothing specifically female about the bonnet. It does, however, seem to be associated with the androgynous attractions of Adonis. Ronsard admires his mistress

> Quand d'un bonnet sa teste elle adonise,
> Et qu'on ne sçait s'elle est fille ou garçon,
> Tant sa beauté en tous deux se desguise.

"Amours de Cassandre" XCIV, *Oeuvres Complètes*, ed. Gustave Cohen, 2 vols (Paris, 1972), I. 40.

golden vision from such recalcitrant raw material, and the speech is a real tribute, if not to Adonis, at least to the power of beauty which, though it cannot change the world, provides imaginative access to a world that is different.

Venus, however, still has to come to terms with the fact that Adonis has been killed by the boar. Her first attempt to account for this involves presenting the boar as an exception to the general rule—an animal who, because his "downward eye still looketh for a grave" (1106), did not see and, therefore, could not respond to the beauty of Adonis. But the force of her Edenic vision is such that it will not allow of exceptions, and so the boar must be made to participate in nature's universal infatuation with the lovely boy:

> "'Tis true, 'tis true; thus was Adonis slain;
> He ran upon the boar with his sharp spear,
> Who did not whet his teeth at him again,
> But by a kiss thought to persuade him there,
>   And, nuzzling in his flank, the loving swine
>   Sheathed unaware the tusk in his soft groin.
>
> Had I been toothed like him, I must confess
> With kissing him I should have killed him first."
> (1111–18)

These lines have given rise to a great deal of comment, much of it arguing that the boar is, in some way, a manifestation of Venus' own destructive lust. But before we follow this line of thought, it is worth remembering that the conceit of the boar attempting to kiss Adonis is an old one, dating back to a late Greek poem that the Renaissance attributed to Theocritus and that Shakespeare could have known through E. D.'s translation of *Sixe idillia* (1588). Shakespeare, in any case, does not give the conceit anything like the prominence it is accorded by Tarchagnota (1550) who allows the boar an eloquent speech of self-defense which wins the pardon of the goddess. The plain and primary sense of the passage is that Adonis has been killed not by lust but by accident. The desire of Venus would have killed Adonis only if she had been toothed like the boar. The purpose of Venus is not to suggest her own guilt by association with the boar, but to make the boar innocent by association with herself.

If Venus, in anticipation, saw the assault of the boar as violent sexual aggression (661–66), that is not the way she sees it now. The "angry chafing boar" has become "the loving swine" whose tenderness and innocence are condensed into the verb "nuzzling." It seems rather perverse to take a passage where Venus absolves the boar from any aggressive intention and use it to prove that he embodies her own destructive instincts.

Venus concludes the first part of her lament with a reflection on the blessing she has failed to obtain:

> "But he is dead, and never did he bless
> My youth with his, the more am I accursed."
> (1119–20)

The formulation is characteristically disingenuous. It would allow the hearer to assume that only the accident of death—and not the resistance of Adonis—has deprived Venus of satisfaction. "My youth with his" suggests a generational equality that has been belied both by her own claims to experience and by her repeated infantilization of Adonis. "Accursed" foreshadows the curse that she will soon place on love: one can almost hear the unspoken antimetabole "Love is accursed and thus she curses love."

Venus falls to the ground (the last of her many falls in the poem) and "stains her face with his congealèd blood" (1122). It sounds rather like a ritual gesture of mourning by which the goddess shares in the grief of nature, imitating the plants that "stole his blood, and seemed with him to bleed" (1056). The sense of ritual is strengthened by the solemn and formal movement of anaphora and parison at the beginning of the following stanza.

> She looks upon his lips, and they are pale.
> She takes him by the hand, and that is cold.
> She whispers in his ears a heavy tale,
> As if they heard the woeful words she told.
>   (1123–26)

Venus is taking leave of the beauties of Adonis one by one, gathering up echoes of "Touch but my lips with those fair lips of thine" (115), "Full gently now she takes him by the hand" (361) and "For to a pretty ear she tunes her tale" (74). As if anticipating the burial that would normally follow this formal leave-taking, the imagery becomes heavily funereal:

> She lifts the coffer-lids that close his eyes,
> Where lo, two lamps burnt out in darkness lies.
>   (1127–28)

The context implies the paronomasia "coffer-coffin," thus suggesting how death has transformed the caskets that once held the jewels of Adonis' eyes. The eyes themselves become like the candles that, after the funeral service, have guttered out in the darkness of the crypt. But if eyes are lamps (as at 489, "Were never four such lamps together mixed"), they are also mirrors as Venus herself had insisted when urging Adonis to see his beauty reflected in her eyes (119). Now it is Venus who tries and fails to find herself in the eyes of Adonis:

> Two glasses, where herself herself beheld
> A thousand times, and now no more reflect.
>   (1129–30)

The epizeuxis "herself herself" neatly recalls "Narcissus so himself himself forsook" (161). In Venus' grief for Adonis there is an element of frustrated narcissism which explains her rage against a world which no longer reflects her own purposes or her own image.

The world has not ended with the life of Adonis, and Venus rages that, for all her efforts to identify him with the sun, "the day should yet be light" without him (1134). There remains, however, one aspect of her earlier prophecy that she can attempt to fulfill. She can call down "black chaos" (1020), if not on the world at large, at least on that domain over which she is assumed to hold sway.

> "Since thou art dead, lo, here I prophesy
> Sorrow on love hereafter shall attend."
> (1135–36)

The details of the prophecy or curse (1135–64) need not detain us long. The rhetorical devices are relatively simple and appropriately formal, consisting mainly of anaphora ("It shall" nine times), antitheses (at least a dozen) and chiasmus. Venus relies on a long tradition of poems about the contradictory effects of love, of which Petrarch's *S'amor non è* and *Pace non trovo* (*Canzoniere*, 132 and 134) were probably the most popular examples.[15] But whereas the Petrarchan tradition usually maintains some balance between positive and negative effects (love wounds and heals, debases and exalts, brings sweetness and bitterness, provokes civil war and is the only source of peace, etc.), Venus is eager to show that, in the long run, "all love's pleasure shall not match his woe." Thus even apparently positive elements are given a negative gloss. For example, love may "strike the wise dumb, and teach the fool to speak," but this is not so much a recognition of love's power to confer eloquence as a declaration that love silences wisdom and broadcasts folly. Or again

> "It shall be merciful, and too severe,
> And most deceiving when it seems most just."
> (1155–56)

---

[15] See Anthony Mortimer, *Petrarch's Canzoniere in the English Renaissance* (Milan and Bergamo, 1975), 56–61.

Love's mercy here is not a welcome relief from the sufferings it inflicts, but rather a deceptive trick designed to keep the lover in a permanently unstable condition. If this is Petrarchism, it is Petrarch tasted through the bitter filter of Wyatt where even reassurance contributes to uncertainty ("Assured I doubt I be not sure").

Venus concludes her curse as she began it by linking the future of love to her own past.

> "Sith in his prime death doth my love destroy,
> They that love best their loves shall not enjoy."
> (1163–64)

The prophecy of Venus seems like an instruction to read the whole poem as an etiological myth which explains how love came to be the way it is. Yet Venus, in fact, stands etiology on its head since she proclaims that from now on love will be for others what it already has been for her. It is a procedure that cries out for the poem's characteristic figure of antimetabole: by warning that she will make love unhappy Venus shows how unhappy love has made her. In much the same way Genesis implies that man is sinful because of his separation from God and that he is separated from God because he has sinned. Shakespeare brings into the open what is, perhaps, the underlying problem of all etiological myths—that what purports to be an account of the cause turns out to be a description of the effect.

The conclusion of *Venus and Adonis* must have presented Shakespeare with a considerable challenge. For most of the poem he had been careful to avoid direct confrontation with his source for the tale in the *Metamorphoses*, Book X. It is not simply that he omits all the antecedents that Ovid provides and that he modifies the whole situation by making Adonis resist the advances of the goddess. The striking fact is that most of the frequent Ovidian echoes seem to derive from almost anywhere in the *Metamorphoses* except the passage that gave him the story in the first place. The sexually aggressive female

160 VARIABLE PASSIONS

and the reluctant youth recall Salmacis and Hermaphroditus (IV. 285–388) and, to a lesser extent, Echo and Narcissus (III. 339–510); the Lament of Venus owes little to Ovid's goddess, but a great deal to his long line of desperately eloquent human heroines (including those of the *Heroides*); the episode of Mars and Venus harks back to Book IV (171–89); even the description of the boar takes its details not from the boar of Book X but from the Calydonian boar of Book VIII. Shakespeare, while happy to plunder the riches of the *Metamorphoses*, is not writing the kind of paraphrase, adaptation or expansion that keeps sending his readers back to the original.

At the close of the poem, however, direct confrontation would be inevitable. However much of the Ovidian story Shakespeare might choose to omit, the final metamorphosis had to remain; and here, if anywhere, readers would be waiting to compare and to judge. Shakespeare needed to provide a metamorphosis that would rival Ovid in virtuosity while remaining coherent with his own rereading of the myth.

The challenge, it must be said, was formidable. This is Ovid in his most dazzling form and the passage must be given in full if we are to appreciate the significance of Shakespeare's modifications.

"at non tamen omnia vestri
iuris erunt" dixit. "luctus monimenta manebunt
semper, Adoni, mei, repetitaque mortis imago
annua plangoris peraget simulamina nostri;
at cruor in florem mutabitur. an tibi quondam
femineos artus in olentes vertere mentas,
Persephone, licuit: nobis Cinyreius heros
invidiae mutatus erit?" sic fata cruorem
nectare odorato sparsit, qui tactus ab illo
intumuit sic, ut fulvo perlucida caeno
surgere bulla solet, nec plena longior hora

>   facta mora est, cum flos de sanguine concolor ortus,
>   qualem, quae lento celant sub cortice granum,
>   punica ferre solent; brevis est tamen usus in illo;
>   namque male haerentem et nimia levitate caducum
>   excutiant idem, qui praestant nomina, venti.
>   (*Met*, X. 724–39)

"But all shall not be in your [the Fates'] power. My grief, Adonis, shall have an enduring monument, and each passing year in memory of your death shall give an imitation of my grief. But your blood shall be changed to a flower. Or was it once allowed to thee, Persephone, to change a maiden's form to fragrant mint, and shall the change of my hero, offspring of Cinyras, be grudged to me?" So saying, with sweet-scented nectar she sprinkled the blood; and this, touched by the nectar, swelled as when clear bubbles rise up from yellow mud. With no longer than an hour's delay a flower sprang up of blood-red hue such as pomegranates bear which hide their seeds beneath the tenacious rind. But short-lived is their flower; for the winds from which it takes its name shake off the flower so delicately clinging and doomed easily to fall.

Ovid's conclusion to the story is finely balanced between consolation and regret. Venus establishes an annual ritual (the Adoniazusae) to commemorate the death of her lover, but she has no power to grant him anything like a full-blown apotheosis and even the metamorphosis she does perform has to be justified with the precedent of Persephone and Menthe. She does, however, bring into being a flower that will continue to embody both his beauty and his fragility. The last two lines, with the wonderfully mimetic suspension of the syntax and the final sighing exhalation of *venti*, leave us with the consolation that beauty, in some form or other, will always be renewed and with the regret that its specific incarnations will always prove transient.

In turning to Shakespeare, the first thing we notice is that his Venus is incapable of offering Adonis even the limited version of perpetuation granted in the *Metamorphoses*. Where Ovid's Venus challenges the Fates ("all shall not be in your power"), Shakespeare's goddess seems strangely passive. That there should be no suggestion of an annual commemoration is consistent with the tone of the preceding speech: a communal rite of mourning would, after all, be a way of coming to terms with death and a gesture of solidarity that this vindictive Venus is in no mood to make or accept. Even more important is the fact that in Shakespeare the metamorphosis of Adonis appears as a natural miracle which owes nothing to the intentions or powers of the goddess:

> By this, the boy that by her side lay killed
> Was melted like a vapour from her sight,
> And in his blood that on the ground lay spilled
> A purple flower sprung up, chequered with white.
> (1165–68)

"By this" is typical of the poem's rapid transitions and indicates succession with no necessary suggestion of causality—especially since Venus, in the preceding speech, has made no reference to metamorphosis. This goddess, therefore, has no power over the natural world and the metamorphosis appears less as a consolation for the death of Adonis than as the final stage of the process that takes him from her or a last cruel joke of nature. A number of details confirm that Shakespeare is, in fact, consciously undermining traditional readings of the myth. Not only is there no indication that Adonis embodies the vegetative and seasonal cycle (an aspect that is, in any case, barely perceptible in Ovid), but even the idea that the flower will somehow perpetuate his beauty is frustrated by Venus herself.

> She bows her head the new-sprung flower to smell,
> Comparing it to her Adonis' breath,
> And says within her bosom it shall dwell,
> Since he himself is reft from her by death.
>   She crops the stalk, and in the breach appears
>   Green-dropping sap, which she compares to tears.
> (1171–76)

The gesture, absent in Ovid, is the one she has attributed to death ("thou pluck'st a flower," 946), but it also recalls her own attempt to crop the flower of Adonis' virginity and her argument that flowers should be "gathered in their prime" (131). By now literalizing her own metaphor Venus inverts its significance. The metaphorical cropping of the youth's virginity would have ensured his perpetuation through offspring; the literal cropping of the flower cuts off any hope of regeneration. In this context, it may well be significant that Shakespeare does not identify the flower. Ovid specifies that, though in color it resembles pomegranate, it is, in fact, the flower that takes its name from the wind, the anemone (from Greek *anemos*) that his readers could recognize. By omitting to name the flower Shakespeare may be implying that it no longer exists; its beauty, like that of Adonis, has been lost without trace. We remember that Venus had urged on Adonis the example of "sappy plants" (165), but here the "green-dropping sap" of the Adonis–flower falls to the earth like wasted semen.

Shakespeare clearly modifies Ovid's account by depriving the metamorphosis of its consolatory function. The spirit of the whole passage remains, however, characteristically Ovidian, involving as it does the dissolution of a human identity followed by the subject's reemergence in a radically simple form reflecting the status to which he or she has been reduced by the story. As Leonard Barkan remarks, "the artistic effect of metamorphosis is to transform human identities into images."[16] Thus, to take only one example, the transformation of Arachne into a spider (*Met*, VI. 1–145) eliminates all that made her an individual—her lowly birth, her professional pride, her irreverence towards the gods—and makes her simply an embodiment of skill in weaving. Shakespeare's Adonis receives the same kind of treatment. Not only is the complex adolescent we have known reduced to a single image of beauty, but, in conformity with the role assigned to him throughout the poem, it is a beauty that will not be reproduced.

---

[16] Barkan, 26.

Since Venus herself has not performed the metamorphosis, she remains uncertain as to how it should be understood. The radical ambivalence of her gesture in cropping the flower is reflected in a final speech that hovers between a recognition that it is no real perpetuation of Adonis and a desire to cherish it as his child.

> "Poor flower," quoth she, "this was thy father's guise—
> Sweet issue of a more sweet-smelling sire—
> For every little grief to wet his eyes.
> To grow unto himself was his desire,
>   And so 'tis thine; but know it is as good
>   To wither in my breast as in his blood.
>
> "Here was thy father's bed, here in my breast.
> Thou art the next of blood, and 'tis thy right.
> Lo, in this hollow cradle take thy rest;
> My throbbing heart shall rock thee day and night.
>   There shall not be one minute in an hour
>   Wherein I will not kiss my sweet love's flower."
>   (1177-88)

The two stanzas complete Venus' rewriting of the story and offer a culminating image in which the Adonis-flower becomes both the child that Adonis has not given her and the lover that he has never been. Jonathan Bate has argued persuasively that the image of the son who takes his father's place in the mother's bed is an "adroit variation" on the Myrrha story in Ovid.

> Ovid begins his tale with Adonis as a son issuing from a tree. Shakespeare ends his with a flower issuing from Adonis who thus becomes a father. Shakespeare's Venus acts out an extraordinary family romance. By imaging her lover as a father, she makes herself into the mother and the flower into the fruit of their union. But the

logic of the imagery dictates that the flower is her sexual partner as well as her child, for it clearly substitutes for Adonis himself.[17]

The birth of Adonis was the result of an incestuous father-daughter union (Cinyras and Myrrha); Venus exploits his death and metamorphosis to envisage a further incest which is that of mother and son. But even without reference to the Myrrha story it would still be clear that an incest is the only conclusion that can satisfy the goddess's desire to possess Adonis both as child and as lover. Throughout the poem she has alternated between bouts of sexual aggression and moments of maternal protectiveness: she leaves us with the only image that can reconcile her "variable passions."

Venus exploits the power that the living usually have over the dead, that of being able to transform them into self-flattering fictions. The Adonis-flower, unlike Adonis himself, cannot answer back to say that he is no longer a child and will not be a lover. We may doubt, however, whether Venus is really convinced by her own rhetoric. The consolation involved in seeing the flower as the child of Adonis is countered by her memory of the Adonis who refused procreation despite her argument that "things growing to themselves are growth's abuse" (166):

> "To grow unto himself was his desire,
> And so 'tis thine, but know it is as good
> To wither in my breast as in his blood."
> (1180–82)

This, surely, is a recognition that the metamorphosis must be ultimately meaningless. Even cradled at her breast, the flower will still wither and is, therefore, no real perpetuation of Adonis. As Clark Hulse remarks, "narratively, he must die to become that flower, and what the flower means is that he must die."[18] Only ironically can the flower be made to

---

[17] Bate, 58–59.
[18] Hulse, 153.

resemble Adonis by being rendered barren and there is a touch of the same vindictiveness that produced her prophetic malediction on love. Because Adonis himself has vanished without trace, she condemns the flower to the same extinction. She had warned Adonis against the blind brutality of the boar who "would root these beauties as he roots the mead" (636); now that her worst fears have been realized she takes revenge on the world by attempting to crop whatever beauty remains. We remember that Venus had started out by describing Adonis as "The field's chief flower" (8), and had gone on to demonstrate an extraordinary facility in all forms of analogy, "Applying this to that, and so to so" (713). But Shakespeare, as John Kerrigan has argued, is acutely conscious of the dangers of "false compare,"[19] and in *Venus and Adonis* most of the elaborate analogies that the goddess constructs end up by working against her. Venus' vindictive cropping of the flower is provoked by her recognition that nothing is really comparable with the unique and irreplaceable beauty of Adonis. It is her way of saying "You alone are you" (Sonnet 84), her farewell to analogy.

It is finally disgust with the world that gains the upper hand over the illusory consolations of the metamorphosis:

> Thus, weary of the world, away she hies,
> And yokes her silver doves, by whose swift aid
> Their mistress, mounted, through the empty skies
> In her light chariot quickly is conveyed,
>   Holding their course to Paphos, where their queen
>   Means to immure herself, and not be seen.
>   (1189–94)

The couplet, as Roe suggests,[20] may contain an echo of Virgil:

---

[19] John Kerrigan, introduction to his edition of *The Sonnets and A Lover's Complaint*, New Penguin Shakespeare (Harmondsworth, 1986), 18–33.

[20] Roe, 138.

> ipsa Paphum sublimis abit sedesque revisit
> laeta suas, ubi templum illi centumque Sabaeo
> ture calent arae sertisque recentibus halant.
> *(Aen*, I. 415–17)

> She herself through the sky goes her way to Paphos, and joyfully revisits her abode, where the temple and its hundred altars steam with Sabaean incense and are fragrant with garlands ever fresh.

If Shakespeare is indeed inviting comparison with the Virgilian passage, then our attention is drawn to the difference between the condition of the goddess in his poem and her very different status in the epic. Virgil's Venus leaves her son, Aeneas, with words of encouragement after demonstrating her power to protect him; Shakespeare's Venus leaves Adonis whom she regards as the son she has been unable to protect. Aeneas is destined to become the father of a great race; Adonis has no progeny. In the *Aeneid* Venus flies away in a joyful spirit to receive the homage of her devotees and to be greeted with "garlands ever fresh;" in *Venus and Adonis* she is "weary of the world," "means to immure herself" and carries a flower that will wither at her breast. For Virgil's Venus divinity carries with it a power to change the world; for Shakespeare's goddess divinity offers, at best, an escape from the world that she cannot change.

There is, of course, also a flight to Paphos (Cyprus) in the *Metamorphoses*. Venus takes off after warning Adonis against the dangers of hunting and is recalled in mid-flight by the groans of the dying youth (*Met*, X. 717–20). Thus Ovid's story ends not with Venus abandoning the world, but with her returning to it, accepting her share of grief and offering the consolation of an annual ritual and a metamorphosis. Shakespeare's Venus has nothing to offer the world except her curse. Ovid's version ends with a goddess who stands on earth, sharing our common human experience of transience and loss; but Shakespeare's goddess has already been all too human—frustrated, sweating and repeatedly falling to the ground. Being a creature of extremes, she reacts by a rejection of humanity. It is because her descent has been so complete that her ascent sounds so unconditional.

These comparisons with Virgil and Ovid might lead us to think that *Venus and Adonis* ends with the desolate vision of a world deprived of divine sympathy or protection, overarched by "the empty skies" and abandoned to the arbitrary violence of the boar. One doubts, however, whether many readers have left the poem under such a cloud. Any sense of gloom is surely dispelled by the grace, swiftness and lightness of the imagery. There is, if anything, a sense of relief in seeing the goddess restored to her supernatural element of freedom, space and soaring flight, finally released from the gravity that bound her to earth and to the human condition. We respond this way because we too are released from gravity, freed from any temptation to read this ending as the conclusion to a real human tragedy. The burden of pathos that might have been imposed on us by seeing Venus as a *mater dolorosa* is lifted by this magical Venus whose silver doves draw her chariot through the skies. We need not feel too sorry for someone who can so easily shake off the weight of the world and we are, indeed, slyly encouraged to think that her protestations of eternal devotion to the memory of Adonis should be taken with a pinch of salt. We are not told that she will, in fact, "immure herself, and not be seen," only that she "means" to do so. Shakespeare does not go so far as Ronsard who, in his "Adonis," reminds us that Venus will soon console herself with the Phrygian shepherd, Anchises *(Telles sont et seront les amitiez des femmes)*,[21] but there is a hint of the same urbane cynicism.

Shakespeare's handling of the conclusion works on two levels. On the one hand, as we have seen, he undermines the positive significance of the metamorphosis as a perpetuation of beauty or as a myth of seasonal regeneration; on the other hand, he clears the atmosphere and lightens the spirit by finally restoring the poem to the realm of fable.

---

[21] Ronsard, ii. 33.

The last stanza throws light on some of the assumptions that underlie Shakespeare's handling of his Ovidian source. For all the portentous interpretations of classical myth offered by assorted Neoplatonists and iconographers (some of them still return to plague interpretation of the poem), the Ovidian revival of the sixteenth century did not lend itself to solemnity and in this it was faithful to the spirit of Ovid himself. Though an occasional allegorical gloss might come in handy to deflect censorship, there is little evidence that Lodge, Marlowe, Shakespeare, Drayton and other authors of *epyllia* regarded classical mythology in general or the *Metamorphoses* in particular as a repository of universal wisdom.

Given the gravity with which modern criticism usually uses the term "myth," it might be better to follow common Renaissance practice and to speak of the Ovidian stories as "fables"—fables which allowed poets to treat potentially serious sexual themes without committing themselves to seriousness. The ending of *Venus and Adonis* is consistent with this attitude. It is designed to distance the reader from the often hilarious but frequently uncomfortable psychological realism of the poem. The real and final metamorphosis is that of a frustrated woman and a sullen youth into miraculous apparitions who vanish in the turning of a verse. Adonis is "melted" from our sight and Venus disappears into "the empty skies." The whole story—so convincingly represented, so solidly embodied, so fraught with the potentialities of comedy and tragedy—dissolves like the masque in *The Tempest*, freeing us to regard as entertainment the disturbing passions it has entertained.

5

Shakespeare and the Italian Tradition of Venus and Adonis

I

The only significant source for Shakespeare's *Venus and Adonis* is Ovid's *Metamorphoses*, both in Latin and in the Golding translation, but he would certainly have been familiar with the two great traditions of Ovidian interpretation. That of the Renaissance mythographers from Boccaccio onwards was available in such English texts as Thomas Cooper's *Thesaurus* (1565) and Abraham Fraunce's *Third part of the Countesse of Pembrokes Yvychurch* (1592), to say nothing of *The Faerie Queene*, Book III. The alternative tradition of *Ovide moralisé* would have been transmitted to him through a variety of channels including Golding's own prefatory verse epistle and, most probably, his own first exposure to the *Metamorphoses* at grammar school. It is highly unlikely, if not quite impossible, that Shakespeare knew any of the sixteenth-century continental Adonis poems and, though he might have learned from someone like Florio that the topic was especially popular in Italy, he would hardly have needed to look to any Italian poem for instruction. As F. T. Prince has remarked, "the Elizabethans idolized their Ovid, and they did not need to know much Italian to absorb the intention and the methods of the numerous Italian poets who set out to expand and modernize the same type of material."[1] It does not, however, follow that the Italian tradition is irrelevant to Shakespeare's poem. It is relevant not because it provides us with some previously unsuspected source, but because it allows us to look at the range of potentialities that Ovid's story offered to Renaissance poets: a comparison and analysis of the specific choices made should illuminate what is distinctive and personal in Shakespeare's version.[2]

The most immediately striking aspect of Ovid's tale, as compared with almost all Renaissance versions, is its brevity. If we exclude the long insert-story of Hippomenes and Atalanta which is introduced on the most fragile of pretexts (*Met*, X. 560–704), we are left with no more than 76 lines (X. 519–59, 705–39) for Venus and Adonis. Yet it may well have been precisely Ovid's immensely suggestive condensation of situations, the sense of a scenario waiting to be filled out, that proved such an irresistible temptation to the Renaissance taste for *copia*. It will, therefore, be useful to list the *nuclei* of the Ovidian narrative.

> Venus, accidentally scratched by Cupid's arrow, falls in love with Adonis (X. 519–28).
>
> Venus abandons her usual haunts (including Heaven) and, dressed like Diana, goes hunting with Adonis (X. 529–41).
>
> Reclining with Adonis in an idyllic landscape, Venus warns him against the hunting of wild beasts (X. 542–59, 705–07).

---

[1] Prince, p. xxx.

[2] A useful article covering some of the same material is Paolo Cherchi, "Molte Veneri e pochi Adoni—con un inedito attribuibile a G. B. Strozzi," *Esperienze letterarie*, XIII, 1988, 15–38. Cherchi is, however, mistaken in regarding Tarchagnota's poem as the first Italian version of the Adonis myth. His aim, in any case, is to provide a context for Strozzi's poem rather than Shakespeare's.

Insert-story of Hippomenes and Atalanta (X. 560–704).

Venus leaves for Cyprus (Paphos). Adonis ignores her warning, wounds the boar and receives his own death-wound in the groin (X. 708–16).

Recalled by the groans of Adonis, Venus laments and reproaches the Fates. She establishes an annual ritual in memory of her lover and transforms his blood into the anemone (X. 717–39).

What this summary omits is, of course, the particular context given to the Adonis myth in the *Metamorphoses*. Book X presents an extraordinary range of transgressive or unconventional sexual situations. Its narrator is Orpheus who, rejecting women, has taught the Thracians the love of tender boys (X. 83–85). After announcing his topic as "boys beloved of gods and maidens inflamed by unnatural love and paying the penalty for their lust" (X. 152–54), he tells of Jove's passion for Ganymede, the love of Phoebus for Hyacinthus, the origin of prostitution with the Propoetides, the strange infatuation of Pygmalion with his statue and, in the longest episode of the book (X. 298–518), Myrrha's incestuous desire for her father Cinyras which results in the birth of Adonis. We shall see how the Italian poets varied in their reactions to a context that inevitably shed a disturbing and sinister light on a tale that they exploited primarily for its combination of eroticism and pathos.

Paraphrases of the *Metamorphoses* had been circulating in Italy since the late fifteenth century, but the fashion for *ottava rima* versions seems to have been set by Niccolò degli Agostini, an imitator of Boiardo, with his *Tutti i libri di Ovidio Metamorphoseos* (1522). The prolific and versatile humanist Lodovico Dolce (1508–68) translated the first book into unrhymed verse in 1539, but had been converted to *ottava rima* by the time his complete version emerged as *Le trasformationi* (1553). But the text that points to the future success of the Adonis story in particular happens to be a side-product of Dolce's activity as an Ovidian translator, his *Stanze nella favola d'Adone* (1545).[3] Some of the eighty-three stanzas are lifted almost without modification from *Le trasformationi*, but there is an important innovation in Dolce's transposition of Ovid's story into the mode of Renaissance pastoral. In Ovid the idyllic setting receives only a brief recognition from Venus herself:

> sed labor insolitus iam me lassavit, et, ecce,
> opportuna sua blanditur populus umbra,
> datque torum caespes: libet hac requiescere tecum.
> (X. 554-56)

But now I am aweary with my unaccustomed toil; and see, a poplar, happily at hand, invites us with its shade, and here is grassy turf for couch. I would fain rest here on the grass with you.

Dolce expands this into a full-blown *locus amoenus*, a meadow ringed with myrtles, a perfect temperate climate, a clear fountain, abundant fruit and flowers, swallows and nightingales, nymphs and shepherds (sts. 4–13). And yet the whole is veined with melancholy. Mysterious voices sing a *carpe diem* refrain and recall the sad fate of Narcissus and Echo; the flowers in the garden are all born of tragic metamorphosis:

> Era quel luogo al fine adorno e pieno
> Di quanti fior giamai creò Natura;
> Ch'in tal forma d'human corpo terreno
> Cangiati fur da strana empia ventura.
> (st. 11)

---

[3] I have used the second edition, *Il Capitano, comedia di M. Lodovico Dolce, con la favola d'Adone*, Venice, 1547.

That place was filled and adorned with as many flowers as Nature had ever created; which, from a human earthly body, had been changed into such a form by strange and evil chance.[4]

Not only is the destiny of Adonis prefigured by the flowers, but his problematic sexual status is suggested both by comparison with Hyacinthus, Ganymede and the Alexis of Virgil's *Eclogue* II, and by the fact that he looks like the twin brother of Cupid (sts. 14–15). That the lover of Venus should be the double of her son and that his beauty should have such a distinctly homoerotic appeal is enough to remind us of the ill-fated incestuous and homosexual passions that play such a large part in the *Metamorphoses*. For all the pastoral paraphernalia, we are still in a very Ovidian world.

As in Ovid (X. 532), Venus has abandoned Heaven to stay with her lover: rather than stay without him "she would renounce a thousand heavens and her own divinity" (*Cangeria mille cieli, e l'esser diva*). For Ovid this means only that she has to accompany Adonis in his hunting; for Dolce, in keeping with his pastoral modification, it involves the transformation of a goddess into a shepherd's wife who sleeps on a hard and dusty bed, milks the goats and ewes with her celestial hands, shears the sheep and weaves wicker baskets to hold the cheese (sts. 17–22). If Ovid gets a malicious pleasure from seeing Venus dressed as Diana (X. 536), Dolce obviously relishes giving her an even more incongruous role as patroness of cottage industry.[5]

---

[4] All translations of the Italian Adonis poems are my own.

[5] Ronsard will pick this up in his "Adonis" (1563). Ronsard, ii. 27.

> O bien-heureux enfant! donc la belle Cythère,
> La mère des Amours, à toy seul veut complaire!
> Seulette avecques toy veut tondre les brebis,
> Et de sa blanche main leur pressurer le pis,
> Et te baisant mener les boeufs au pasturage,
> Esclisser des paniers, et faire du froumage.

176 VARIABLE PASSIONS

Dolce's pastoral interlude occupies the first 25 stanzas of his poem, after which he reverts to the Ovidian narrative with the warning against wild beasts and the insert-story of Hippomenes and Atalanta (sts. 26–46). Dolce departs from Ovid in providing a cause for Adonis' death in Juno's moral outrage at his mother's incest; but this, in fact, results in an Ovidian paraphrase as Juno recounts (without the sympathy of Orpheus) the story of Myrrha and Cinyras (sts. 52–63). In the Lament (sts. 75–82) there are some details (Venus deploring her own immortality and envying Persephone who will inherit Adonis in Hades) that have been taken from the Greek tradition as represented by Bion's "Lament for Adonis," but the final metamorphosis is little more than a paraphrase of Ovid.[6]

Apart from its pastoralism, Dolce's poem is still very much the story as Ovid tells it. Five years later came Giovanni Tarchagnota's *L'Adone* (1550), a poem of roughly the same length (74 stanzas of *ottava rima*) which makes more radical modifications and incorporates further elements from the Greek tradition.[7] Tarchagnota begins with Venus preparing to leave for Paphos and, haunted by a vague foreboding, warning Adonis against wild beasts (sts. 1–5). No sooner has the goddess departed than Adonis hears the noise of the approaching boar and takes arms against it. This occasions a first allusion to his origin with the suggestion that "perhaps to punish Myrrha and her crime, he [the boar] came towards her son so horribly" (*Che forse per punir Mirra, e 'l suo errore, / Venia verso il figliuol con tanto orrore*). For Ovid it was not the boar who punished Myrrha by killing her son, but Adonis who took revenge on Venus for provoking his mother's passion (*Met*, X. 524). But here, as in Dolce's introduction of an offended Juno, there is an attempt to find some

---

[6] For Bion and also for the pseudo-Theocritean idyll mentioned later, see A. S. F. Gow, *The Greek Bucolic Poets* (Cambridge, 1952).

[7] *L'Adone di M. Giovanni Tarchagnota*, Venice, 1550. Reprinted in Angelo Borzelli, *Il Cavalier Giambattista Marino* (Naples, 1898), 307–24.

motive for the death of Adonis which Ovid presents as a straightforward hunting accident. Another cause for the catastrophe is provided when Tarchagnota makes Adonis wound the Boar (sts. 19–20) with the same arrow of Cupid that had scratched Venus. Thus the boar becomes enamored of Adonis and, inflamed by the sight of his naked thigh, rushes to embrace him and accidentally gives him a mortal wound. Already we are beginning to see the multiplication of motives that will eventually blur the simple outlines of Ovid's story.

Adonis laments his fate (sts. 27–31), but proclaims that he will still possess "infinite glory and consummate pleasure" (*gloria infinita, sommo gioir*) if his death elicits from Venus a single tear or a sigh. Venus returns and, as in Ovid, tears her hair, beats her breast and reproaches the Fates. The captured boar obtains forgiveness by protesting that his sole desire was to kiss Adonis, and expiates his crime by burning off his offending tusks. Venus decides to take her lover's body to Paphos where she will create the Garden of Adonis and establish an annual ritual in his memory. As she transforms his blood into a flower, her own hairs that she has torn from her head take root and grow into a plant that bears her name (presumably, the maidenhair fern, *adiantum capillus-veneris*). The poem concludes with the wry observation that Venus is now so devoted to tending her garden that lovers "do not too often feel the goddess near them in their need" (*Onde i devoti non troppo spesso / Sentir ne' lor bisogni nume presso*).

We still have the basic scheme of Ovid's story, but Tarchargnota's considerable debt to the Greek tradition can be seen in the importance he attaches to the Lament of Venus. In Ovid there is no real lament; we are simply told that Venus reproaches the Fates before we pass directly to her creation of the ritual and to the metamorphosis. Bion's poem gives the actual Lament twenty lines (42–61) which Tarchagnota multiplies by four (sts. 43–59). It is obviously to Bion rather than to Ovid that we owe the Renaissance tendency to develop the Lament of Venus, somewhat at the expense of the metamorphosis, into a kind of secular *pietà*, almost a sub-genre which hardly needs the support of a narrative frame. Minor details taken from Bion (the multitude of winged loves, the elaborate toilette bestowed on the corpse of Adonis) need not concern us here. Tarchagnota's most remarkable non-Ovidian move is his emphasis on the boar's love for Adonis which he develops from an anonymous late Greek poem that the Renaissance attributed to Theocritus as Idyll 30. The same conceit appears in a Latin epigram by Minturno, in Saint-Gelais and, of course, in Shakespeare; but only Tarchagnota makes it a central element in his narrative. As for the disturbing ancestry of Adonis, the idea that Venus and the boar are both wounded by Cupid's arrow allows the poet to evoke the Ovidian context of transgressive loves while deflecting excessive moral outrage. The arrow exemplifies that *potenza incredibile d'Amore* which links the love of gods for humans (Venus and Adonis) with that of beasts for humans (the boar and Adonis) and that of humans for beasts (Pasiphae and the bull). In that light, the incest of Myrrha, though one of those "strange ardours" that Nature condemns, hardly seems like an exception to the rule.

> Fu ben strano l'amor di lei, che in Creta
> Un bianco toro amando arse cotanto:
> Fu strano, che giacer potesse lieta
> Mirra madre d'Adon col padre a canto:
> Fur simili ardor strani, perchè il vieta
> Natura; e pentir sol ne segue, e pianto:
> Ma chi di ciò gran maraviglia prende,
> Poi che l'amante vi discorre, e intende?
> (st. 17)

Most strange was her love who in Crete burned so hotly for the love of a white bull; strange was it that Myrrha, mother of Adonis, could lie happily with her father: such ardors were strange because Nature forbids them; and from them follows only remorse and weeping: but who can be greatly surprised at this since the lover speaks of it and understands?

The stanza spells out the implications of Ovid's vision of love as an experience where the extraordinary becomes the norm.

Tarchagnota clearly works to make the myth more self-contained than it is in either Ovid or Dolce. The antecedent Myrrha story receives only passing reference and is irrelevant to the outcome, while the insert-story of Hippomenes and Atalanta is omitted entirely. At the same time the internal coherence of the poem is reinforced by symmetrical patterning: Adonis has his own lament to balance that of Venus, there is a double metamorphosis (the blood of Adonis and the hair of Venus), and the arrow that sets the story in motion also brings it to an end. This may be Ovidian poetry, but it is no longer Ovidian paraphrase.

In his 54-stanza *Favola d'Adone* (1553) Girolamo Parabosco (c. 1524-57) reduces the action to a strict minimum.[8] From the balcony of Heaven Venus sees the sleeping Adonis and, wounded by Cupid's arrow, descends to earth to become his lover. Called away to Paphos on a flying visit to attend a feast in her honor (*divinité oblige*), she utters her expected warning (sts. 33-35) the inefficacy of which is underlined by the fact that her catalogue of dangerous animals includes the tiger, the bear, the wolf and the lion, but omits the boar. There follows, as always, the death of Adonis, the Lament and the metamorphosis—this last liquidated in a single stanza. The story is almost completely severed from the antecedents provided in the *Metamorphoses*: there is no reference to Myrrha and only the most fleeting allusion to Hippomenes and Atalanta when Venus cryptically reminds Adonis that the lion is her old enemy. Parabosco, in fact, evacuates as many narrative elements as he can and hurries over those that remain to leave us with a structure where the intervention of the boar splits the poem into two almost autonomous sections—the first an erotic idyll (the lovemaking of Venus and Adonis) and the second a

---

[8] For Parabosco's poem I have used *Quattro libri delle lettere amorose di M. Girolamo Parabosco* (Venice, 1561).

female complaint (the Lament of Venus). This structure, with its corresponding double vision of Venus as seductress and *mater dolorosa*, prefigures Shakespeare's version, though Parabosco lacks Shakespeare's skill in combining contrast with continuity. The first section recalls Dolce's pastoral in some of its details, but the emphasis is significantly different. Where Dolce stresses the humble domestic happiness of the lovers, Parabosco is resolutely erotic and again he prefigures Shakespeare in the sexually aggressive behavior he attributes to Venus. Ovid had, indeed, made it clear that Venus takes the initiative—inevitably, since it is she and not Adonis who is grazed by Cupid's arrow—but the tradition had never called into question the promptness of Adonis' response. Parabosco's Venus has to work surprisingly hard for her satisfaction (sts. 9–17). She finds Adonis sleeping and her flattering address fails to wake him. When, at last, he is aroused by her kissing and shaking, his first reaction is a frightened look and an attempt to run away (*si desta / Timido in vista; e di fuggir procaccia*). Even Venus' reassurance that she does not bite is not enough to overcome the timidity of this virginal youth. Inexperienced in the "sweet lascivious motions of love" (*i dolci d'Amore atti lascivi*), Adonis seems more inclined to worship the goddess than to embrace her. He falls at her feet in adoration and Venus obtains her end only when she takes him in her arms and quite literally opens the way to intercourse, "giving him the entrance and the path to that fair place that every ardent lover craves and desires" (*Dandogli a quel bel loco adito e via / Ch'ogni caldo amator brama e desia*). There is nothing in Ovid, Dolce or Tarchagnota that comes so close to Shakespeare's earthy goddess who will adopt the same tactics without the same success. Parabosco's Adonis, however, does not really share the "leaden appetite" of his English counterpart: in this "sweet game repeated many times" (*iterato più volte il dolce gioco*) we are left in no doubt that, for all his youth and timidity, he has what it takes to satisfy a goddess for whom once is decidedly not enough. The second section, occupied largely by the Lament, is more conventional and adds little to the pattern found in Bion, Dolce and Tarchagnota—except perhaps for a few eruptions of the Petrarchan wordplay (*immortal—martire—morire*) that Shakespeare also will lend to his Venus.

Even more radical in its evacuation of narrative elements is the *Favola di Venere e Adone*, a 40-stanza poem attributed to Giovan Battista Strozzi the Younger (1551–1634) and recently published by Paolo Cherchi.[9] Strozzi begins with a brief praeteritio which makes his exclusions explicit:

> Non voglio or questionar se per vendetta
> La madre Citerea Cupido offese
> Perché Mirra a giacer col padre astretta
> Dal venereo furor infame il rese;
> O se della faretra la saetta
> Avanzar fuor il ferro non comprese,
> Onde le punse non volendo il petto
> Mentr'ei l'abbraccia, ell'a sé 'l tien stretto.
> (st. 3)

> I do not now want to ask whether Cupid harmed his mother Cytherea out of vengeance because Myrrha, compelled by lustful madness to lie with her father, had rendered him infamous; or whether he did not know that from the quiver there pointed the arrowhead with which unawares he wounded her breast while he embraced her and she held him close.

By stanza 5 we have already arrived at the warning which extends through to stanza 27. The death of Adonis occupies only two stanzas and the remainder of the poem comprises the Lament and the metamorphosis. On the surface it would seem as if we have the same two-part structure as in Parabosco; but there is, in fact, no sense of a contrast or of a break between the two parts. Venus, in her warning, already foresees and bewails the death of Adonis so that, as Cherchi

---

[9] The text is provided by Cherchi in the article already cited.

points out, the whole poem appears as one long lament.[10] Even the Ovidian episode of Venus as huntress is incorporated into a female complaint as the goddess protests (My feet are killing me!) that she is not really cut out for this kind of activity:

> Ma come queste delicate piante
> De' miei candidi piè ponno soffrire
> Tra sassi e spini (ohimè) fatiche tante.
> [...]
> Offendo i delicati omeri miei
> Portando tue nodose e gravi reti.
> (sts. 15, 17)

But how can the delicate soles of my white feet suffer such toils (alas!) among stones and thorns. [...] I hurt my delicate shoulders carrying your knotty and heavy nets.

This querulous tone of "Look what I do for you" distinguishes Strozzi's Venus from her predecessors and undermines the traditional idyllic relationship between the lovers. Though Adonis does not, as in Shakespeare, refuse her advances, Venus is forced to recognize that he prefers the toils (*aspre fatiche*) of hunting to the pleasures (*giocondissimi diletti*) that she has to offer. As the goddess pleads that she is arguing in his interest rather than her own, we hear all the accents of a lovers' quarrel:

> Quant'ella più 'l distoglie, ei più s'incuora
> A seguir l'ostinato suo pensiero.
> Ei timida la chiama; ella s'accora
> E 'l dispregiante accusa animo fiero.
> (st. 27)

---

[10] Cherchi, 25.

The more she dissuades him, the more he resolves to follow his obstinate intention. He calls her cowardly; she is distressed and blames his proud scornful spirit.

One may note in passing that this Venus again displays considerable linguistic ingenuity, playing untranslatable games with the name of Adonis' mother (*Di Mirra no, ma di ria pianta dura*) and with the antanaclasis of *tronco*—the trunk of the myrrh which gave Adonis the life that envious Fate has now "truncated." Strozzi's goddess is not, however, self-conscious in her rhetorical virtuosity, and Adonis is given no direct speech. We are still far from Shakespeare's animated debate where rhetoric itself is called into question. But there is at least the sense that Adonis has a mind of his own and that, perhaps, the void left by the evacuation of narrative incident can be filled by argument as well as by lyrical expansion.

If, as seems probable, Strozzi's poem dates from the turn of the century, it can be seen as something of a throwback. A very different way of handling the Adonis story had already been introduced with the *Metamorfosi d'Ovidio* (1561) of Giovanni Andrea dell'Anguillara (1517–72).[11] Unlike Dolce's *Le trasformationi* which it supplanted, and unlike the Golding version that Shakespeare used, this is not so much a translation as an extended and highly-inventive *ottava rima* paraphrase. Thus the 442 lines that Ovid devotes to the Cinyras-Myrrha and Venus-Adonis tales become 1440 (X, sts. 131–311) in Anguillara. The expansion, however, retains something close to the Ovidian distribution: where Ovid has 221 lines for Cinyras-Myrrha and exactly the same number for Venus-Adonis (if we include the insert-story of Hippomenes and Atalanta), Anguillara gives 84 stanzas to the former

---

[11] I have used *Le Metamorfosi d'Ovidio ridotte da Gio Andrea dell'Anguillara in ottava rima* (Venice, 1585). Two tales from Anguillara were translated by Henry Reynolds: "Ariadne's Complaint" (1628) and "The Tale of Narcissus" (1632). Both are included in Henry Reynolds, *Tasso's 'Aminta' and Other Poems*, ed. Glyn Pursglove (Salzburg, 1991).

and 96 to the latter. It is in the second section that we find a significant modification. Whereas in Ovid the insert-story is almost twice as long as its frame, Anguillara gives Venus and Adonis slightly more space than Hippomenes and Atalanta and this more equitable balance is achieved by introducing a number of non-Ovidian features.

The first of these is not, as we might by now expect, the Lament which Anguillara, following Ovid's example, merely reports in a few lines. It is rather Venus' long wooing speech (X. sts. 224-36) which, unlike the wooing in Parabosco, is less an erotic invitation than a justification of love as the mysterious unity of two in one, the fusion of soul and body and the source of all creation:

> D'ogni cosa creata Amore è padre.
> Or, se, mentre ad amare Amore esorta,
> Fa nascer tante cose alme e leggiadre;
> Ogn'un, ch'al voto suo non è secondo,
> In quel, ch'a lui s'avien, distrugge il mondo.
> (X. st. 224)

Love is the father of all created things. Now, when Love exhorts to love and brings to birth so many fair and lovely things, anyone who refuses to follow his lead destroys the world in himself.

This cosmic view of love is probably the nearest any of the Italian versions get to Spenser's Garden of Adonis where Adonis, as the lover of Venus, becomes "the Father of all forms" (*FQ*, III. vi. sts. 35-50). It also anticipates the arguments of Shakespeare's Venus that the refusal of love is a form of suicide ("So in thyself thyself art made away," 763) and a crime against the order of Nature ("By law of nature thou art bound to breed," 171). To Parabosco's double Venus (seductress and *mater dolorosa*) Anguillara has added another dimension—that of the philosophical Venus who will also find her way into Shakespeare's poem.

Anguillara's major non-Ovidian features, however, involve the addition of narrative incident. In terms of proliferating plots it seems that Anguillara wanted to outdo Ovid in much the same way as Ariosto had outdone Boiardo. Thus Adonis, having reached manhood, returns to his father's kingdom (now Cyprus, not Ovid's Panchaia) and becomes king in his turn. Since the island is sacred to Venus, this provides the occasion for his meeting with the goddess. When Venus leaves it is not to attend her own festival in Paphos, but for Heaven where the gods are to hold a sort of Father's Day celebration in honor of Jove. After her departure, Adonis decides to revisit his birthplace (Sabaea) and, passing through Lebanon, is invited by the king to join a hunting-party. He is then killed by the boar who is an incarnation of the jealous Mars, the rejected lover of Venus. Anguillara devotes relatively little space to these non-Ovidian features, but their presence in his version does suggest a shift in direction. Whereas Dolce and Parabosco had reduced the action to a minimum and Tarchagnota had made it more self-contained, Anguillara initiates a contrary movement where the story undergoes an expansion that is both spatial (the journey of Adonis) and temporal (the antecedents that explain his death). There is obviously an attempt to make good the lack of incident in Ovid's version. That later poets continued to feel Ovid's economy as a problem is suggested by Marcello Macedonio (c. 1575–1620) when he remarks of his own pastoral *Adone* (1614) that it cannot claim the title of tragedy because it is "completely without plot" (*affatto priva di favola*).[12]

In the wake of Anguillara, therefore, the Adonis myth loses the relatively simple outlines imposed by the old blend of Ovid and Bion. The trend may be exemplified by Ettore Martinengo's 1174-line *L'Adone, idillio* (1614) in which Ovid's tale becomes diluted rather than enriched by an unhappy combination of static tableaux and extraneous episodes.[13] An inkling of what awaits us is given by the

---

[12] Cited from Marcello Macedonio, *Le nove Muse* (Naples, 1614) by Giovanni Pozzi in "Metamorfosi di Adone," *Strumenti critici* 16, October 1971, 352.

[13] *L'Adone, idillio di Ettore Martinengo* (Venice, 1614).

opening description of spring. The conventional *chronographia*, which his predecessors (and Shakespeare) cover in a couple of lines or stanzas, is here extended over one bloated sentence (1–47) where a fourfold *allhor che* (like Chaucer's "Whan that") introduces a long sequence of subordinate clauses before we reach the subject (Venus) in line 41. Martinengo then launches into the story of Cinyras and Myrrha (48–200), following Ovid fairly closely but not failing to add the occasional telling detail of his own, as when Cinyras, seeking to comfort his melancholy daughter, inadvertently caresses her breast. Martinengo, however, tends to avoid the direct speech that Ovid exploits to such dramatic effect. Thus Myrrha's appeal to nature against the laws of man (*Met*, X. 329–31) becomes, with an unmistakable echo of Tasso's *Aminta* (669–74), the narrator's own comment:

> O troppo, dura legge;
> Non già legge d'Amor, d'Amor nel regno,
> Non legge di Natura,
> Che la Natura offende;
> Ma legge sol di quel Tiranno onore
> Di natura, e d'Amore.
> (142–47)

O too hard law—not the law of love in the kingdom of love, not the law of nature for it offends nature; but the law only of honor, that tyrant over nature and love.

Given the poem's earlier horror at the betrayal of religion and decency, this could only be justified as an example of free indirect speech or as subtle characterization by the poet of an inconsistent narrator. But one hesitates to credit Martinengo with such sophistication. The avoidance of direct speech is, in fact, only one aspect of his relentlessly non-dramatic approach to the myth. Characterization and narrative rhythm are submerged by passages of descriptive expansion whose primary purpose seems to be that of allowing Martinengo to display his classical erudition. The sixteen lines which Ovid devotes to the miraculous birth of Adonis and his resemblance to Cupid are developed into a vast tableau (201–381) where the hierarchy, geography and botany of the ancient world are ransacked for illustration. A lively military metaphor greets the lovemaking of Venus and Adonis (*Qui si corre all'assalto, e qui si crolla / Con Ariete gentil porta amorosa*; "Here there is rushing to the assault and here the gate of love is broken by the sweet battering-ram"); but this burst of energy soon gives way to another tableau, the long procession that nature brings to contemplate the sleeping lovers (597–723) while, with a nice touch of exoticism, a parrot rehearses the *carpe diem* theme. Though the poem returns to Ovid for Venus as a huntress and for her warning (735–839), the transition to the catastrophe is delayed by an expanded version of the incidents introduced by Anguillara (Adonis as king in Cyprus, his journey to his birthplace). When we are told of the jealousy of Mars (1031–57), it sounds too much like an afterthought to function convincingly as a factor in the plot. The universal mourning of nature provides yet another elaborate tableau and finally there is the Lament— not from Venus but from the narrator himself who rapidly defeats any expectations we may still have by concluding that he cannot describe the feelings of the goddess or the metamorphosis since he is himself overcome with grief:

> Dillo tu Dea d'amore
> E 'l chiuso duol ti disacerba alquanto
> Se però il dir dolente
> Pur come a me, non interrompe il pianto.
> (1163–66)

Say it yourself, Goddess of Love, and may it ease your pent-up sorrow, unless, as in my case, weeping should interrupt the grieving speech.

The disarming modesty of this gesture is hardly enough to overcome our impression of a narrative so diluted by tableaux, so sporadic in its progression, so pulled out of shape, that by this time neither the reader nor the poet himself cares greatly how it comes to an end.

The final dissolution of the Adonis myth is accomplished by the longest poem in Italian literature, the vast *Adone* (1623) of Giambattista Marino (1569–1625). There would be no point here in attempting to describe the extraordinary proliferation of episodes that Marino grafts onto the Ovidian story. One might say that Marino, rather than choosing between different versions of the myth, manages to include them all while elaborating further variants of his own. Thus Cupid, Apollo, Vulcan, Mars, and Diana are all, to some extent, made responsible for the death of Adonis.[14] As an example of what happens to the narrative structure, Giovanni Pozzi cites the episode where Venus falls in love with the sleeping Adonis. Marino gives us three consecutive accounts (III, sts. 16, 17–55, 56–116): the second is a slight variation on the first, while the third is radically inconsistent with the other two. What is true of one episode is true of the poem as a whole which abounds in subtle revisitings and in potentially infinite variations on analogous situations. Pozzi argues that what has often been seen as a mass of brilliant and disorganized digressions is, in fact, the result of a consciously anti-epic design, a structure in which, as in a starry sky, all the units illuminate each other without being related to a single discernible center.[15] It is in this plural and decentered regard,

---

[14] There is no consensus about which of the gods or goddesses is responsible for the death of Adonis, but a strong tradition follows Nonnos (*Dionysiaca*, xli. 204–11) in blaming Mars. For Apollodorus (*The Library*, III. xiv. 4) it is Diana, though there is also a hint that Persephone may be involved since she is the rival of Venus for the possession of Adonis. I have been unable to trace where Dolce found the idea that it was Juno.

[15] Pozzi, 348–49, 355–56. The starry sky as a metaphor for the structure of Marino's *Adone* is cited by Pozzi from Francesco Busenello (1598–1659), an ardent defender of the poem against the attacks of Stigliani. For a detailed discussion of the poem's organization see Giovanni Pozzi's monumental two-volume edition of the *Adone* (Milan, 1976).

with its consequent rejection of conventional narrative logic, that the Adonis myth at last evaporates. It is not, perhaps, a strange destiny for a myth that the Renaissance inherited from the *Metamorphoses* where the sequence of the episodes is less important than the play of contrast and analogy between them and which is also, in its way, an anti-epic.

II

We have seen how, in the national literature that exploited it most fully, the Adonis poem evolves from an initial stage of restriction and self-containment through expansion to final dissolution. Seen in relation to that evolution, Shakespeare's *Venus and Adonis* obviously belongs to the initial stage. Eliminating all antecedents, the poem begins *in medias res* and never looks back. With no insert-story of Hippomenes and Atalanta, no explicit allusion to Myrrha, no jealous Mars and no account of how Venus came to fall in love, the events of the poem can be reduced to the following simple scheme:

    I   Venus with Adonis (1–810)
    IA   The Wooing (1–588)
    IB   The Warning (589–810)

    II   Venus Alone (811–1194)
    IIA The Solitary Night, the Morning Hunt (811–1030)
    IIB Lament and Metamorphosis (1031–1194)

At first sight, this resembles Parabosco's structure of two parts, the first erotic and the second pathetic, with the corresponding and contrasting images of Venus as seductress and *mater dolorosa*. Shakespeare, however, is by no means so schematic. While the Venus of IA urges Adonis to take a masculine initiative, she also abounds in gestures and metaphors that infantilize him so that the maternal Venus of IIA and IIB does not appear inconsistent. Pathos begins to emerge with the warning of IB and reaches a first climax with the ecphrasis of the hunted hare (673–708), but the warning also continues the wooing of IA since Venus uses the threat of the boar as an argument for immediate lovemaking. Thus Shakespeare, unlike Parabosco, establishes a continuity between the erotic and the pathetic by making the warning serve as a bridge between the two. It follows that we get a more complex Venus who does not play first one role and then the other, but who is throughout both threatening and protective, sexually aggressive and maternal. And this, in turn, creates a basic ambivalence about Adonis' response since we are not sure whether surrender to Venus would be an initiation into manhood or a regression to infancy.

Shakespeare's Adonis does not surrender, and it is a conflict not an amorous idyll that is brought to an end by his death. There has been much speculation about where Shakespeare might have found a source for his uncooperative Adonis. Hints of a disdainful Adonis have been unearthed in a number of Shakespeare's contemporaries (Marlowe, *HL*, I. 12–14; Spenser, *FQ*, III. i. sts. 34–38; Greene, *Never Too Late*). We have seen that Parabosco's youth is initially unreceptive and there is, of course, the controversial case, raised by Panofsky, of the Prado Titian which shows Venus clinging to a remarkably burly Adonis who is about to leave her for the hunt.[16] But none of this amounts to much beyond the established tradition that it is Venus who takes the initiative and that she fails to cure Adonis' passion for hunting. Modern editors of the poem are agreed that, if we must find a source for the Adonis

---

[16] Erwin Panofsky, *Problems in Titian, Mostly Iconographic*, New York, 1969, 149–54.

who refuses love, we should look back to the *Metamorphoses*—not to the Venus and Adonis episode, but to the stories of Salmacis and Hermaphroditus (IV. 285–388) and, to a lesser extent, Narcissus and Echo (III. 344–510), both of which concern beautiful youths who refuse the advances of inflamed nymphs. Both stories help Shakespeare to flesh out the rather empty figure who appears in the *Metamorphoses* and in the other Renaissance Adonis poems. Hermaphroditus contributes to the disturbingly androgynous quality of his beauty and Narcissus to his obsession with autonomy and self-knowledge. By taking the unprecedented and yet very Ovidian decision to make Adonis resist, Shakespeare creates a new balance between the protagonists. In Dolce, Parabosco, Strozzi, Anguillara and Martinengo, though we hear Venus at length, Adonis is not given direct speech. Shakespeare redeems him from this passivity and gives him a voice of his own, not as loquacious as that of Venus, but distinctive enough to make him a convincing antagonist.

In *Venus and Adonis* the relative balance between the protagonists means that debate can compensate for the lack of action. What allows the debate to continue over eight hundred lines is the fact that both protagonists keep shifting ground, becoming progressively more inconsistent in the arguments they advance. Thus Venus will, in the same stanza (127–32) claim that Adonis, though unripe, may still be tasted and then conclude that fair flowers should be "gathered in their prime;" Adonis himself will first utter a categorical rejection of love ("My love to love is love but to disgrace it," 412), then immediately suggest that he needs more time to become a satisfactory lover (415–20) and finally argue that what he rejects is not love but lust (787–804). Even the narrator is infected by the inconsistency of the characters he observes, at one moment expressing sympathy for Venus ("Poor queen of love, in thine own law forlorn," 251), at another reproaching her for "careless lust" that forgets shame and honor (556–58), and then promptly lauding her persistence (565–70). We suggested earlier that Italian poets may have been attracted by Ovid's story precisely because its brevity offered so many opportunities for rhetorical expansion. This would also hold good for Shakespeare, but the difference lies in the way the rhetoric itself is called into question. Both protagonists are aware that the situation betrays them into a language which is not their own. Venus remarks "Unlike myself thou hear'st me moralize" (712) and Adonis concludes his sermon on lust and love with the admission that "The text is old, the orator too green" (806). As for the efficacy of rhetoric as a means of persuasion, we are constantly reminded that, though Venus can excite herself into action, Adonis is detained not by her eloquence but by her physical strength. The comedy arises both from the display of a rhetoric that convinces no-one but its user and from the incongruity between the elegance of what Venus says and the crudity of what she does. The point is not, as Adonis would have us believe, that Venus uses rhetoric as a mere cover for brute appetite. "The sea hath bounds, but deep desire hath none" (389) and what we are asked to recognize is that neither verbal nor physical gesture can ever make knowable an emotion that defies expression as it defies definition.

To this questioning of the status and efficacy of rhetoric should be added another element that would have been more obvious to Shakespeare's first readers than it is to us. Since the tradition provided no precedent for the resistance of Adonis, the rhetorical assault of Venus would have involved a suspense completely lacking in the orthodox Italian versions. Would Venus succeed in seducing Adonis? Here, at least, was one aspect of the story not given in advance. While Shakespeare might seem, at first sight, to follow the Italian tradition which exploits the story for rhetorical rather than narrative invention, in fact he overcomes the distinction by making the success or failure of rhetoric an issue in the plot.

We have already traced the variety of solutions that Italian poets provide to the problem of antecedents and insert-stories in the *idillio*. Dolce recounts both Cinyras-Myrrha and Hippomenes-Atalanta as insert-stories; Tarchagnota, Parabosco and Strozzi give them only passing reference; Anguillara restores them to their Ovidian status;

Martinengo begins with Cinyras-Myrrha, but has only a one-line allusion to Hippomenes-Atalanta; both Anguillara and Martinengo introduce a variety of non-Ovidian episodes. Shakespeare, as we have seen, adopts the most rigorous policy of exclusion and yet, because monotony obviously does threaten a narrative so poor in events (*affatto priva di favola*), he provides a structural equivalent to insert-stories with three passages that are not so much episodes as ecphrases. These are Venus' recall of her affair with Mars (97–114), the interlude of the horses (259–34), and Venus' evocation of the hunted hare (679–708). The first of these suggests that lovemaking with Venus would be less a conquest for Adonis than a threat to his virility; the second casts a skeptical light on the conventional theme of lovemaking as a "natural" activity; the third, while following Ovid in proposing the hare as a more suitable prey than the boar, seems to undo its purpose by exciting sympathy for the victim who is implicitly being offered up as a substitute for Adonis. Shakespeare, therefore, is sensitive to the structural problems of the genre (epyllion or *idillio*) and recognizes that *copia* alone is not enough to maintain interest in a basically static situation. His ecphrases, however, unlike the insert-stories of the Italian versions, do not require the pretext of narrative explanation. Their function is not to answer questions (How did Venus fall in love with Adonis? Why does she hate wild beasts? Who is responsible for the death of Adonis?), but to create a mature, witty and ironic vision of the motives, issues and arguments that divide the protagonists.

The *locus amoenus* features, to a greater or lesser extent, in almost all the Italian Adonis poems. Dolce and Martinengo offer the most elaborate setpieces on the backdrop of lush grass, perfumed flowers, melodious birds, shady trees, clear fountains and fluttering Cupids; but Tarchagnota, Parabosco and Macedonio are not without their *fiorite valli, piagge amene, alati Amori*, and other standard features of *l'adorno Giardin d'Amor*. Shakespeare avoids anything like a formal *topographia* and yet the setting permeates the whole poem. Ever since Coleridge and Keats readers have been impressed by the freshness and accuracy of the poem's natural imagery which conveys the sense of a landscape that has been rendered deliberately unmythological not only by becoming so recognizably English, but also by being peopled with such small and humble creatures as the divedapper, the caterpillar and the snail. Despite invigorating moments like the exultant freedom of the horses, the song of the lark or the golden glory of the second sunrise, this is no *locus amoenus*. With its repeated images of animal violence and suffering, Shakespeare's poem comes closer than any of the Italian versions to the naturally dangerous landscape of the *Metamorphoses* where the murderous eruption of the boar needs no explanation in terms of a special supernatural conspiracy. The only *locus amoenus* that the poem allows us to envisage is that of Venus' own landscaped body (229–40), the defiant rhetorical creation of a goddess who will learn all too well what to expect from nature.

The one major non-Ovidian feature that Shakespeare shares with almost all the Italian versions is the extended Lament of Venus (1069–1120, 1133–64). Shakespeare might seem to have made the task more difficult for himself by first indulging in a parody of the female complaint (829–52), but he rises to this self-imposed challenge by transforming the Lament into a complex dramatic monologue that brings together all the goddess's contradictory motives and self-deceptions. By avoiding all allusion to her own aggression and Adonis' determined resistance, she rewrites the whole story in a way that satisfies her incurable vanity. Whereas Tarchagnota and the pseudo-Theocritean poem had made the boar plead love for Adonis in his own defense, Shakespeare gives the same conceit an entirely new function by placing it in the mouth of Venus herself as a last desperate attempt to believe in the innocence of a nature that has betrayed her. This at the same time as she places a curse on the world for failing to live up to her expectations. In most Italian Adonis poems the final metamorphosis tends to fall rather flat. It is, in fact, given somewhat perfunctory treatment—as if, after all the emotion invested in the Lament, it could only be anti-climactic. Shakespeare overcomes the difficulty by radically changing the significance of the metamorphosis which is now no longer a transformation that Venus performs but one that she is obliged to interpret in a closing speech where her need for self-flattering fictions clashes with her recognition of ultimate defeat.

Looking back over *Venus and Adonis*, it is clear that Shakespeare is working in the genre that the Italians knew as the *idillio*. He exploits the same blend of eroticism and pathos and even his comedy can be seen to have Italian precedents if one thinks of Dolce's Venus as housewife or of the seduction scene in Parabosco. At a formal level also Shakespeare conforms to the dominant Italian pattern with a basic two-part structure, ecphrases that correspond to the insert-stories, set speeches that display rhetorical virtuosity and an un-Ovidian extended Lament. At the level of plot, however, Shakespeare rewrites the relation between Venus and Adonis as a conflict, and this fundamental modification provides his version with an unprecedented density and unity since all the traditional features of the Adonis *idillio* are harnessed to a new function as psychological indicators. Thus the *locus amoenus* is no longer the setting of the poem but a piece of erotic self-advertisement, the affair with Mars and the boar's infatuation with Adonis are presented not as explanations for the catastrophe but as Venus' own self-flattering and self-consoling fictions, the Lament becomes her final attempt to rewrite the story, and the metamorphosis is significant not in mythic terms as a promise of rebirth or renewal but for the extraordinarily revelatory reaction it provokes in a goddess who needs to redefine her relation to the human world. Above all, though Shakespeare exploits the rhetorical *copia* characteristic of the genre, the effect is rarely one of gratuitous ornamentation and there is little of the conventional prettiness that we find in Italian Adonis poems. Shakespeare starts out by restoring rhetoric to its primary function as persuasion and this allows him to demonstrate, throughout the poem, an ironic consciousness that rhetorical strategies can be simultaneously impressive and unconvincing, inevitable and misguided, misleading and self-revealing. Through this mature and sophisticated treatment, a story that was already hackneyed in Italian literature becomes the springboard for a new wave of Ovidian poetry in England. In Sonnet 76 the poet wryly admits to keeping "invention in a noted weed": to read *Venus and Adonis* in the light of the Italian tradition is to marvel at just how much invention one noted weed could be made to contain.

Bibliography

This bibliography provides a fairly comprehensive list of the scholarly material on *Venus and Adonis* published since Hyder Edward Rollins's *The Poems: A New Variorum Edition* (1938).

With a few exceptions, I have omitted general Shakespearean criticism and major sixteenth and seventeenth-century English poems; but I include all French and Italian texts cited for purposes of comparison.

Texts of the Poem

Evans, Maurice, *The Narrative Poems*, New Penguin Shakespeare (Harmondsworth, 1989).

Maxwell, J. C., *The Poems*, The New Shakespeare (Cambridge, 1965).

Prince, F. T., *The Poems*, Arden Shakespeare (London, 1960).

Roe, John, *The Poems*, New Cambridge Shakespeare (Cambridge, 1992).

Rollins, Hyder Edward, *The Poems: A New Variorum Edition of Shakespeare* (Philadelphia, 1938).

Wells, Stanley, and Gary Taylor, *The Oxford Shakespeare* (London, 1986).

Secondary Material

Akrigg, G. P. V., *Shakespeare and the Earl of Southampton* (London, 1968).

Allen, D. C., "On Venus and Adonis" in *Elizabethan and Jacobean Studies, Presented to F. P. Wilson*, ed. H. Davis and H. Gardner (Oxford, 1959), 100–11.

Allen, Walter, Jr., "The Non-Existent Classical Epyllion", *SP* 55 (1958), 515–18.

Asals, Heather, "*Venus and Adonis*: The Education of a Goddess," *SEL* 13 (1973), 31–51.

Austin, Henry, *The Scourge of Venus* (London, 1613).

Baldwin, T. W., *William Shakspere's Small Latine and Lesse Greeke* (2 vols., Urbana, Ill., 1944).

——————, *On the Literary Genetics of Shakspere's Poems and Sonnets* (Urbana, Ill., 1950).

Barkan, Leonard, *The Gods Made Flesh: Metamorphosis and the Pursuit of Paganism* (New Haven, Conn., 1986).

Barksted, William, *Mirrha, the Mother of Adonis; or Lustes Prodegies* (London, 1607).

Bate, Jonathan, *Shakespeare and Ovid* (Oxford, 1993).

Baumlin, Tita French, "The Birth of the Bard: *Venus and Adonis* and Poetic Apotheosis," *Southern Illinois Papers on Language and Literature* 26 (1990), 191–211.

Beauregard, D. N., "*Venus and Adonis*: Shakespeare's Representation of the Passions," *Shakespeare Studies* 8 (1975), 83–98.

Belsey, Catherine, "Love as Trompe-l'oeil: Taxonomies of Desire in *Venus and Adonis*," *Shakespeare Quarterly* 40 (1995), 257–76.

Bensimon, Marc, "*Venus and Adonis* de Shakespeare: métamorphose d'une métamorphose," in *La métamorphose dans la poésie baroque française et anglaise*, ed. Gisèle Matthieu-Castellani (Tübingen-Paris, 1980), 195–202.

Bersuire, Pierre, *Metamorphosis Ovidiana moraliter explanata* (Paris, 1509). Garland reprint (London, 1979).

Bowers, A. Robin, "'Hard Amours' and 'Delicate Amours' in Shakespeare's *Venus and Adonis*," *Shakespeare Studies* 12 (1979), 1–23.

Bowers, R. H., "Anagnoresis or the Shock of Recognition in Shakespeare's *Venus and Adonis*," *Renaissance Papers* (1962), 3–8.

Bradbrook, M. C., *Shakespeare and Elizabethan Poetry* (London, 1951).

——————, "Beasts and Gods: Greene's *Groats-Worth of Witte* and the Social Purpose of *Venus and Adonis*," *Shakespeare Survey* 15 (1962), 62–72.

Brodeau, Victor, *Poésies*, ed. Hilary M. Tomlinson (Geneva, 1972)

Brown, Huntingdon, "*Venus and Adonis:* The Action, the Narrator and the Critics," *Michigan Academician* 2 (1969), 73–87.

Bullough, Geoffrey (ed.), *Narrative and Dramatic Sources of Shakespeare* (8 vols., London, 1957–75).

Bush, Douglas, *Mythology and the Renaissance Tradition in English Poetry* (1932, rev. edn., New York, 1963).

Butler, C. and A. Fowler, "Time Beguiling Sport: Number Symbolism in Shakespeare's *Venus and* Adonis" in *Shakespeare 1564–1964*, ed. Harold Bloom (Providence, RI, 1964).

Cantelupe, E. B., "An Iconographical Interpretation of *Venus and Adonis*, Shakespeare's Ovidian Comedy," *Shakespeare Quarterly* 14 (1963), 141–51.

Cartari, Vincenzo, *Le Imagini de i dei de gli antichi* (Venice, 1571).

Cherchi, Paolo, "Molte Veneri e pochi Adoni," *Esperienze letterarie* 13 (1988), 15–38.

Coleridge, S. T., *Coleridge's Shakespearean Criticism*, ed. T. M. Raysor, (2 vols., London, 1960).

—————, *Biographia Literaria*, ed. J. Shawcross (2 vols, London, 1954).

Cousins, A. D., "Venus Reconsidered: the Goddess of Love in *Venus and Adonis*," *Studia Neophilologica* 66 (1994), 197–207.

Daigle, Lennet, "*Venus and Adonis*: some traditional contexts," *Shakespeare Studies* 13 (1980), 31–46.

Degli Agostini, Niccolò, *Tutti i libri di Ovidio Metamorphoseos* (Venice, 1522).

Dell'Anguillara, Giovanni Andrea, *Le Metamorfosi d'Ovidio ridotte in ottava rima* (Venice, 1584).

Desportes, Philippe, *Diverses Amours et autres oeuvres meslées*, ed. V. E. Graham (Geneva, 1963).

Dickey, Franklin M., *Not Wisely but Too Well* (San Marino, Cal., 1958).

Doebler, John, "The Reluctant Adonis: Titian and Shakespeare", *Shakespeare Quarterly* 33 (1982). 480–90.

—————, "The Many Faces of Love: Shakespeare's *Venus and Adonis*," *Shakespeare Studies* 16 (1983), 33–43.

—————, "*Venus and Adonis*: Shakespeare's Horses", in *Images of Shakespeare*, ed. Werner Habicht and others (Newark, Delaware, 1988), 64–72.

Dolce, Lodovico, *Il Capitano, comedia, con la favola d'Adone* (Venice, 1547).

—————, *Le Trasformationi* (Venice, 1568). Garland reprint, (London, 1979).

Donaldson, Ian, "Adonis and his Horse," *NQ* New Series 19 (1972), 123–25.

Donno, Elizabeth Story (ed.), *Elizabethan Minor Epics* (London, 1963).

───────, "The Epyllion," in *Sphere History of Literature in the English Language, Vol. 2, English Poetry and Prose 1540–1674*, ed. Christopher Ricks (London, 1970), 82–100.

Dowden, Edward, *Shakspere: A Critical Study of his Mind and Art* (London, 1875).

Dubrow, Heather, *Captive Victors: Shakespeare's Narrative Poems and Sonnets* (Ithaca, NY, 1987).

───────, and Richard Strier (eds.), *The Historical Renaissance* (Chicago, 1988).

Duncan-Jones, Katherine, "Much Ado with Red and White: the Earliest Readers of Shakespeare's *Venus and Adonis*," *RES* New Series, XLIV, No 176 (1993), 480–501.

Dundas, Judith, "Shakespeare's Imagery: Emblem and the Imitation of Nature," *Shakespeare Studies* 16 (1983), 45–56.

───────, "Wat the Hare, or Shakespearean Decorum," *Shakespeare Studies* 19 (1987), 1–15.

Empson, William, *Essays on Shakespeare*, ed. David B. Pirie (1986).

Evans, Maurice, *English Poetry in the Sixteenth Century* (London, 1955).

Fienberg, Nona, "Thematics of Value in *Venus and Adonis*," *Criticism: A Quarterly for Literature and the Arts* 31 (1989), 21–31.

Fraenkel, Hermann, *Ovid: A Poet between Two Worlds* (Berkeley and Los Angeles, 1945).

Fraunce, Abraham, *The Third Part of the Countesse of Pembrokes Yvychurch* (London, 1592). Garland reprint, 1976).

Fresnaie, Vauquelin de la, *Foresteries* (1555), ed. Marc Bensimon (Geneva, 1956).

Galinsky, G. Karl, *Ovid's Metamorphoses* (Oxford, 1975).

Gent, Lucy, "*Venus and Adonis*: The Triumph of Rhetoric," *MLR* 69 (1974), 721–29.

Golding, Arthur, *Shakespeare's Ovid being Arthur Golding's Translation of the Metamorphoses*, ed. W. H. D. Rouse (1904, reprint, London, 1961).

Gow, A. S. F., *The Greek Bucolic Poets* (Cambridge, 1952).

Greenblatt, Stephen, *Shakespearean Negotiations: The Circulation of Social Energy in Renaissance England* (Oxford, 1988).

Greene, Thomas M., *The Light in Troy: Imitation and Discovery in Renaissance Poetry* (New Haven, Conn., 1982).

Greenfield, Sayre N., "Allegorical Impulses and Critical Ends: Shakespeare's and Spenser's Venus and Adonis," *Criticism* 36 (1994), 475–98.

Griffin, Robert J., "'These Contraries Such Unity Do Hold': Patterned Imagery in Shakespeare's Narrative Poems," *SEL* 4 (1964), 43–55.

Guthmüller, B., *Ovidio Metamorphoseos vulgare. Formen und Funktionen der volksprachlichen Wiedergabe klassischer Dichtung in der italienischen Renaissance* (Boppard am Rhein, 1981).

Hamilton, A. C., *The Early Shakespeare* (San Marino, Cal., 1967).

Hart, Jonathan, "'Till Forging Nature Be Condemned of Treason': Representational Strife in *Venus and Adonis*," *Cahiers Elisabethains* 36 (1989), 37–47.

Harwood, Ellen Aprill, "*Venus and Adonis*, Shakespeare's Critique of Spenser," *Journal of the Rutgers University Library* 39 (1977), 44–60.

Hatto, A. T., "*Venus and Adonis*—and the Boar", *MLR* 41 (1946), 353–61.

Hazlitt, William, *Characters of Shakespeare's Plays* (London, 1906).

Howard, Jean E., "Crossdressing, the Theatre and Gender Struggle in Early Modern England", *Shakespeare Quarterly* 39 (1988), 418–40.

Hughes, Ted, *Shakespeare and the Goddess of Complete Being* (London, 1992).

Hulse, Clark, *Metamorphic Verse: The Elizabethan Minor Epic* (Princeton, NJ, 1981).

Jackson, Robert S., "Narrative and Imagery in Shakespeare's *Venus and Adonis*," *Papers of the Michigan Academy of Science, Arts, and Letters* 43 (1958), 315–20.

Jahn, J. D., "The Lamb of Lust: The Role of Adonis in Shakespeare's *Venus and Adonis*," *Shakespeare Studies* 6 (1970), 11–25.

Jardine, Lisa, *Still Harping on Daughters. Women and Drama in the Age of Shakespeare* (Brighton, 1983).

Kahn, Coppelia, "Self and Eros in *Venus and Adonis*," *Centennial Review* 4 (1976), 351–71.

Keach, William, *Elizabethan Erotic Narratives: Irony and Pathos in the Ovidian Poetry of Shakespeare, Marlowe and their Contemporaries* (New Brunswick, NJ, 1977).

Keats, John, *The Letters of John Keats,* ed. Hyder Edward Rollins (2 vols., Cambridge, Mass., 1958).

Kermode, J. F., *Shakespeare, Spenser, Donne: Renaissance Essays* (London, 1971).

Kerrigan John (ed.), *Motives of Woe: Shakespeare and 'Female Complaint': A Critical Anthology* (Oxford, 1991).

———, Introduction to *Shakespeare: The Sonnets and a Lover's Complaint*, New Penguin Shakespeare (Harmondsworth, 1986).

Kiernan, Pauline, "Death by Rhetorical Trope: Poetry Metamorphosed in *Venus and Adonis* and the *Sonnets*," *RES* 46 (1995) 475–501.

Kintgen, Eugene R., *Reading in Tudor England* (Pittsburgh, 1996).

Klause, John, *"Venus and Adonis*: Can We Forgive Them?," *SP* 85 (1988), 353–77.

Kolin, Philip C. (ed.), *Venus and Adonis: Critical Essays* (New York, 1997).

Lake, James H., "Shakespeare's Venus: An Experiment in Tragedy," *Shakespeare Quarterly* 25 (1974), 351–55.

Lanham, R. A., *The Motives of Eloquence: Literary Rhetoric in the Renaissance* (New Haven, Conn., 1976).

Le Doeuff, Michèle, *Vénus et Adonis suivi de Genèse d'une catastrophe* (Paris, 1986).

Leech, Clifford, "Venus and her Nun: Portraits of Women in Love by Shakespeare and Marlowe," *SEL* 5 (1965), 247–68.

Leishman, J. B. (ed.), *The Three Parnassus Plays* (London, 1949).

Lerner, Laurence, "Ovid and the Elizabethans" in *Ovid Renewed*, ed. Charles Martindale (Cambridge, 1988), 121–35.

Lever, J. W., "Shakespeare's Narrative Poems" in *A New Companion to Shakespeare Studies*, ed. K. Muir and S. Schoenbaum (Cambridge, 1971).

——————, "Venus and the Second Chance," *Shakespeare Survey* 15 (1962).

Lewis, C. S., *English Literature in the Sixteenth Century, Excluding Drama* (Oxford, 1954).

Lindheim, Nancy, "The Shakespearean *Venus and Adonis*," *Shakespeare Quarterly* 37 (1986), 190–203.

Macedonio, Marcello, *Le nove Muse* (Naples, 1614).

Marino, Giambattista, *Adone*, ed. Giovanni Pozzi (2 vols, Milan, 1976).

Martindale, Charles and Michelle (eds.), *Shakespeare and the Uses of Antiquity: An Introductory Essay* (London, 1990).

Martindale, Charles, and Colin Burrow, "Clapham's *Narcissus*: A Pre-Text for Shakespeare's *Venus and Adonis*," ELR 22 (1992), 147–75.

Martinengo, Ettore, *L'Adone, idillio* (Venice, 1614).

Maslen, Rob, "*Venus and Adonis* and the Death of Orpheus," *The Glasgow Review. Renaissance* 1 (1993).

Miller, P. W. "The Elizabethan Minor Epic," *SP* 55 (1958), 31–38.

Miller, Robert P., "Venus, Adonis and the Horses," *ELH* 19 (1952), 249–64.

————, "The Myth of Mars's Hot Minion in *Venus and Adonis*," *ELH* 26 (1959), 470–81.

Mortimer, Anthony, "Shakespeare and the Italian Tradition of Venus and Adonis," *Colloquium Helveticum* 22 (1995), 93–116.

————, "The Ending of *Venus and Adonis*," *English Studies* 78 (1997), 334–41.

————, *Petrarch's Canzoniere in the English Renaissance* (Milan and Bergamo, 1975).

Muir, Kenneth, *Shakespeare the Professional* (London, 1973).

————, and Sean O'Laughlin, *The Voyage to Illyria* (London, 1937).

Otis, Brooks, *Ovid as an Epic Poet* (2nd edn., Cambridge, 1970).

Ovid, *Metamorphoses*, with translation by Frank Justus Miller, Loeb Classical Library (2 vols, London, 1977).

Ovide moralisé, Poème du commencement du quatorzième siècle, ed C. de Boer, *Verhandelingen der Koninklijke Akademie van Wetenschappen* (Amsterdam), Afd. Letterkunde, new series XV (1915), XXI (1920), XXX (1931), XXXVII (1936), XLIII (1938). Sändig reprint (Vaduz, 1988).

Palmatier, M. A., "A Suggested New Source in Ovid's *Metamorphoses* for Shakespeare's *Venus and Adonis*," *HLQ* 24 (1961), 163–69.

Panofsky, Erwin, *Problems in Titian, Mostly Iconographic* (New York, 1969).

Parabosco, Girolamo, *Quattro libri delle lettere amorose* (Venice, 1561).

Parker, Patricia, *Literary Fat Ladies: Rhetoric, Gender, Property* (London, 1987).

Parry, Hugh, "Ovid's *Metamorphoses*: Violence in a Pastoral Landscape," *Transactions of the American Philological Association* 95 (1964), 268–82.

Pegg, Barry, "Generation and Corruption in Shakespeare's *Venus and Adonis*," *Michigan Academician* 8 (1975), 105–15.

Petrarca, Francesco, *Canzoniere*, ed. Gianfranco Contini (Turin, 1964).

Pozzi, Giovanni, "Metamorfosi d'Adone," *Strumenti critici* 16 (1971), 336–56.

Price, Hereward T., "The Function of Imagery in *Venus and Adonis*," *Papers of the Michigan Academy of Science, Arts, and Letters* 31 (1945), 275–97.

Putney, Rufus, "*Venus and Adonis*: Amour with Humor," *PQ* 20 (1941), 533–48.

―――, "Venus Agonistes," *University of Colorado Studies* 4 (1953), 52–66.

Rabkin, Norman, *Shakespeare and the Common Understanding* (New York, 1967).

Rebhorn, Wayne A., "Mother Venus: Temptation in Shakespeare's *Venus and Adonis*," *Shakespeare Studies* 11 (1978), 1–19.

Reynolds, Henry, *Tasso's 'Aminta' and Other Poems*, ed. Glyn Pursglove (Salzburg, 1991).

Ronsard, Pierre de, *Oeuvres complètes*, ed. Gustave Cohen (2 vols., Paris, 1958).

Saint-Gelais, Mellin de, *Oeuvres complètes de Melin de Sainct-Gelays*, ed. Prosper Blanchemain (2 vols., Paris, 1873).

Sandys, George, *Ovid's Metamorphosis Englished, Mythologiz'd, and Represented in Figures* (London, 1632).

Segal, Charles Paul, "Landscape in Ovid's *Metamorphoses*," *Hermes: Zeitschrift für Klassische Philologie* 23 (1969).

────────, *Poetry and Myth in Ancient Pastoral: Essays on Theocritus and Virgil* (Princeton, NJ, 1981).

Seznec, Jean, *The Survival of the Pagan Gods: The Mythological Tradition and its Place in Renaissance Humanism and Art* (Princeton, NJ, 1953).

Sheidley, William E., "'Unless It Be a Boar': Love and Wisdom in Shakespeare's *Venus and Adonis*," *MLQ* 35 (1974), 3–15.

Smith, Bruce, *Homosexual Desire in Shakespeare's England* (Chicago, 1991).

Smith, G. Gregory, *Elizabethan Critical Essays* (2 vols., Oxford, 1904).

Smith, Gordon Ross, "Mannerist Frivolity and Shakespeare's *Venus and Adonis*," *Hartford Studies in Literature* 3 (1971), 1–11.

Smith, Hallett, *Elizabethan Poetry: A Study in Conventions, Meaning and Expression* (Cambridge, Mass., 1952).

Spencer, Hazelton, "Shakespeare's Use of Golding in *Venus and Adonis*," *MLN* 44 (1929), 435–37.

Streitberger, W. R., "Ideal Conduct in *Venus and Adonis*," *Shakespeare Quarterly* 26 (1975), 285–91.

Tarchagnota, Giovanni, *L'Adone* (Venice, 1550), reprinted in Angelo Borzelli, *Il Cavalier Giambattista Marino* (Naples, 1898), 307–24.

Tasso, Torquato, *Jerusalem Delivered*, tr. Edward Fairfax (London, 1600).

Thomson, J. A. K., *Shakespeare and the Classics* (London, 1952).

Velz, J. W., "The Ovidian Soliloquy in Shakespeare," *Shakespeare Studies* 18 (1986), 1–24.

Vendler, Helen, *The Art of Shakespeare's Sonnets* (Cambridge, Mass., 1997).

Vickers, Brian, *In Defence of Rhetoric* (Oxford, 1988).

———, *Appropriating Shakespeare: Contemporary Critical Quarrels* (New Haven, Conn. 1993).

Virgil, *Eclogues, Georgics, Aeneid*, with translation by H. R. Fairclough, Loeb Classical Library (2 vols., London, 1974).

Watkins, W. B. C., *Shakespeare and Spenser* (Princeton, NJ, 1950).

Watson, D. G., "The Contrarieties of *Venus and Adonis*," *SP* 75 (1978), 32–63.

Whitaker, V. K., *Shakespeare's Use of Learning* (San Marino, Cal., 1953).

Wilkinson, L. P., *Ovid Recalled* (Cambridge, 1955).

Williams, Gordon, "The Coming of Age of Shakespeare's Adonis," *MLR* 78 (1983), 769–76.

Wind, Edgar, *Pagan Mysteries of the Renaissance* (London, 1958).

Woodbridge, Linda, *Women and the English Renaissance. Literature and the Nature of Womankind* (Brighton, 1984).

Wyndham, George, Introduction to *The Poems of Shakespeare* (London, 1898).

Yoch, James J., "The Eye of Venus: Shakespeare's Erotic Landscape," *SEL* 20 (1980), 59–71.

Zocca, Louis R., *Elizabethan Narrative Poetry* (New Brunswick, 1950).

Index

Rhetorical terms have been included for the convenience of readers who may wish to look up Shakespeare's use of a particular figure. Tales from the *Metamorphoses* are listed under Ovid. Thematic indications are to be found under *Venus and Adonis*.

Adoniazusae, 161
adynaton, 151
Akrigg, G. P. V., 2n2
Allen, Don Cameron, 21n33
Allen, Walter, 6n11
anadiplosis, 152
anaphora, 54, 70, 92, 156, 158
Angeriano, Girolamo, 120n6
antanaclasis, 183
antimetabole, 46, 84, 87, 90, 93, 95, 144, 152, 156, 159
antistasis, 86
antithesis, 30-31, 38, 48-49, 54, 64, 80, 84, 87, 95, 128, 134, 140, 144, 158
Antony and Cleopatra, 46, 48, 154
Apollodorus:
 The Library, 188n14
aposiopesis, 71, 141
Aquinas, St Thomas, 9
Ariosto, Lodovico, 185
Aristotle, 9
Asals, Heather, 11
asyndeton, 61
Augustine, St, 9
Austin, Henry:
 The Scourge of Venus, 67

Baldwin, T. W., xi, 10
Barkan, Leonard, 22n34, 163
Barksted, William:
 Mirrha, the Mother of Adonis, 67
Barnfield, Richard:
 Cynthia, 92n22
Bate, Jonathan, ix, 4, 6, 67, 100, 137, 139, 164-65
Baumlin, Tita French, 17
Beaumont, Francis:
 Salmacis and Hermaphroditus, 7
Belsey, Catherine, ix, 32n41
Bembo, Pietro, 11
Bersuire, Pierre:
 Metamorphosis Ovidiana moraliter explanata, 99n24
Bible:
 Isaiah, 154
 Matthew, 123
Bion:
 Lament for Adonis, 176-78, 180, 185
Bishop, Sir Henry Rowley, 136n3
Boccaccio, Giovanni:
 Genealogia Deorum, 20n32, 171
Boiardo, Matteo, 173, 185
Botticelli, Sandro, 62

210 INDEX

Bradbrook, Muriel, 1n1
Brodeau, Victor, 120n6
Burghley, William Cecil, 1st Baron, 2
Burrow, Colin, 2n2
Busenello, Francesco, 188n15
Bush, Douglas, 13-15, 81n19
Butler, Christopher, 38n2

captatio benevolentiae, 45
carpe diem, 61, 174
Cartari, Vincenzo, 20n32
Castiglione, Baldassarre, 11
Catullus, 61, 96
Chaucer, Geoffrey, 186
Cherchi, Paolo, 172n2, 181
chiasmus, 59, 64, 90, 95, 158
chronographia, 186
Clapham, John:
  Narcissus, 2n2
climax (gradatio), 91
Coleridge, S. T., 3-4, 8, 34, 37, 47, 131-32, 136n3, 193
Comes, Natalis, 20n32
Cooper, Thomas:
  Thesaurus, 20n32, 171
copia, 19, 47, 96, 134, 172, 193, 195
correctio (epanorthosis), x, 141

Daigle, Lennet, 12
Dee, Dr. John, 143
Degli Agostini, Niccolò:
  Tutti i libri d'Ovidio Metamorphoseos, 173
Dell'Anguillara, Giovanni:
  Le metamorfosi d'Ovidio, 183-89
Desportes, Philippe, 41
Diana (Cynthia), 24, 115, 119-22, 172, 175, 188
Dolce, Lodovico:
  Le trasformationi, 173, 183
  Stanze nella favola d'Adone, 174-189
Donne, John:
  "The Canonization", 100
  "Elegy: To his Mistress Going to Bed", 72

  "The Good Morrow", 60
Donno Elizabeth Story, 3n3
Dowden, Edward, 81n19
Drayton, Michael:
  Endimion and Phoebe, 7, 169
Dubrow, Heather, ix, 4, 31n40, 53n6, 71n12
Duncan-Jones, Katherine, ix, 3n4

ecphrasis, 23, 58, 77-80, 193, 195
E. D.:
  Sixe idillia, 155
E. K., x
Elizabeth, Queen, 3n4
ellipsis, 71
epanorthosis (correctio), x, 141
epiplexis, 141
epistrophe, 54
epizeuxis, 64, 104, 157
epyllion, 6-10, 72, 116, 169, 193
etiology, 33, 99, 159
Evans, Maurice, 147n10

Fable of Ovid treting of Narcissus, 6
Fairfax, Edward, 80
Female Complaint, x, 133-35, 180, 194
Ficino, Marsilio, 10-11
Field, Richard, 2
Fielding, Henry:
  Joseph Andrews, 13
Fletcher, Phineas:
  Venus and Anchises, 7
Florio, John, 171
Fowler, Alastair, 38n2
Fraunce, Abraham:
  Third Part of the Countesse of Pembrokes Yvychurch, 20n32, 101, 120n6, 171

Gent, Lucy, ix
Golding, Arthur, 6, 8, 99, 112, 171, 183
Gombrich, E. H., 10
Gow, A. S. F., 176n6
gradatio (climax), 91

Greene, Robert:
 Groats-worth of Witte, 1-2
 Never Too Late, 190
Gresham, James:
 The Picture of Incest, 67

Hatto, A. T., 113-14
Hazlitt, William, 14-16, 149
Henry IV (Falstaff), 13, 74, 96
Hesiod, 2
Homer, 2, 56, 66
homoioteleuton, 93
Horace, 38
Hughes, Ted, 5
Hulse, Clark, 80, 165
hyperbole, 41-42, 47, 62, 96, 115, 119, 125, 137, 146

idillio, 192-95

Jahn, J. D., 55n8, 66n10
Jardine, Lisa, 114n4
Johnson, Dr. Samuel, 15
Jong, Erica, 21
Julius Caesar, 149

Kahn, Coppelia, ix, 4, 29, 88n20
Keach, William, ix, 4
Keats, John, 148, 193
Kermode, Frank, 91n21
Kerrigan, John, xi, 133, 166
Kiernan, Pauline, 81n19
King Lear, 99, 143
Kintgen, Eugene, x
Kristeller, Oscar, 10

Lanham, Richard, ix, 4, 17
Le Doeuff, Michèle, 74
Lewis, C. S., x, 7-8, 13-14, 109
litotes, 87
locus amoenus, 72, 174, 194-95
Lodge, Thomas:
 Scillaes Metamorphosis, 3n3, 7, 169
Love's Labours Lost, 148
Lucrece, 8, 14-16, 134

Lucretius:
 De Rerum Natura, 57

Macbeth, 69, 151
Macedonio, Marcello:
 Adone, 185, 193
Malone, Edmond, 142n8
Marino, Giambattista:
 L'Adone, 185, 188-89
Marlowe, Christopher:
 Hero and Leander, 6, 23, 74, 77n16, 93-94, 110, 169, 190
Martindale, Charles, 2n2
Martinengo, Ettore:
 L'Adone, idillio, 185-88
Maslen, Rob, 30n39
Measure for Measure, 49, 96
meiosis, 87
Menander, 2
Meres, Francis:
 Palladis Tamia, 6
Middleton, Thomas:
 A Mad World, my Masters, 9
mimesis, 80
Minturno, Antonio, 178
Morris, Desmond, 79
Mortimer, Anthony, 158n15

Nonnos:
 Dionysiaca, 188n14
Norbrook, David, 18-19

Othello, 89
Ovid:
 Amores, 1-2
 Ars Amatoria, 77n16
 Heroides, 26, 133, 160
 Metamorphoses, tales:
  Actaeon, 73, 117
  Arachne and Minerva, 21-23, 163
  Atalanta and Hippomenes, 42, 77, 116, 172, 176, 179, 183
  Byblis, 43
  Callisto, 24
  Calydonian boar, 112, 160

Daphne, 24, 138
Dido, 43
Ganymede, 23, 173, 175
Hippolytus, 119, 120n6
Hyacinthus, 173, 175
Io, 24
Mars and Venus, 27, 56-59, 66, 73, 77-78, 90, 155, 160
Medea, 43
Myrrha and Cinyras, 25, 43, 67-69, 130, 164-65, 173, 176, 178-83
Narcissus, 46, 63-64, 150-51, 160, 174, 191
Orpheus, 154, 173
Persephone and Menthe, 161
Phaedra, 43
Propoetides, 173
Pygmalion, 69-70, 173
Salmacis and Hermaphroditus, 99, 160, 191
Tantalus, 56, 110
Ovide moralisé, 8, 56-57, 99, 171
oxymoron, 80, 90, 95, 142

Panofsky, Erwin, 190n16
parables, 123
Parabosco, Girolamo:
 Favola d'Adone, 179-81, 184, 189-90
paradox, 25, 43, 46, 56, 64, 80, 97, 111, 134
parison, 156
paronomasia, x, 38, 153, 157
pathetic fallacy, 135, 150
Pearson, L. E., 8n15
Peend, Thomas:
 Pleasant Fable of Salmacis and Hermaphroditus, 6
Petrarch (Petrarca, Francesco):
 Canzoniere, 126, 158
Petrarchism, 30, 49, 56, 75, 90, 158-59, 181
Plato:
 Symposium, 100
Pliny:
 Natural History, 111

ploke, 64, 87, 140
polyptoton, 38, 54, 11, 140
Pooler, C. K., 116n5
Pozzi, Giovanni, 185n12, 188
praeteritio, 181
Price, Hereward T., 9n16
Prince, F. T., 15-16, 110, 171-72
Putney, Rufus, 13, 23, 104

Return from Parnassus, ix, 9
Reynolds, Henry, 183n11
Reynolds, William, 3n3
Richard II, 74
Roe, John, xii, 12, 121-22, 125, 136, 166
Rollins, Hyder Edward, xi, 3n4, 9n18, 116n5
Ronsard, François, 154n14, 168, 175n5
Ruskin, John, 74

Saint-Gelais, Mellin de, 178
Segal, Charles Paul, 72
Shirley, James:
 Narcissus or the Self-Lover, 3n3
Sidney, Sir Philip:
 Astrophil and Stella, 2, 11, 47
Smith, Bruce, 28
Sonnets, 31, 42-44, 46, 64, 95-97, 123, 127, 153, 166
Southampton, Henry Wriothesly, Earl of, 2-3
Spenser, Edmund:
 Faerie Queene, 3, 9, 20, 56, 80, 100, 171, 184, 190
 Fowre Hymne, 137
 Shepheardes Calender, x
Stigliani, Tommaso, 188n15
Strozzi, Giovan Battista:
 Favola di Venere e Adone, 181-83
synecdoche, 54
systrophe, 141

Tarchagnota, Giovanni:
 L'Adone, 155, 176-80

Tasso, Torquato:
  Aminta, 183n11, 186
  Gerusalemme Liberata, 56, 80
Tempest, 169
Theocritus, 155, 178
Tibullus, 2
Titian, 190
topographia, 193
Troilus and Cressida, 103
Turbervile, George:
  Booke of Hunting, 116
Twelfth Night (Malvolio), 59

Vendler, Helen, xi
VENUS AND ADONIS:
  Allegorical interpretations, 8-12, 56-57, 169
  Androgyny, 41-42, 99-101, 114, 154n14, 191
  Comedy, 13, 22-23, 109-110, 114-15
  Critical reputation, 1-18
  Edenic vision, 45, 50, 72, 154-55
  Equestrian metaphor, 48, 77-79, 89
  Etiology, 33, 159
  Gender roles, 24-29, 41-42, 58-59, 69-70, 75, 85, 92, 112-14, 140
  Incest, 28, 139, 164-65
  Infantilization of Adonis, 27, 45, 102-03, 164
  Landscape, 71-73, 193-94
  Love and lust, 28-33, 127-28, 193-94
  Mobility, 40-44
  Myth and fable, 20-26, 159, 168-69
  Narcissism, 60, 63-64, 154, 157
  Narrative voice, 44-45, 76
  Nature and the norm, 18-19, 26-28
  Neoplatonism, 10-12, 30, 57, 100, 137, 146, 169
  Rhetorical character, 13-20, 29-32, 68, 74-75, 133-34, 191-92, 195-96
  Selfhood and self-knowledge, 31-32, 63-64, 97-98, 151, 191
  Spiral structure, 97

Venus Genitrix, 12, 16, 20, 32
Vere, Lady Elizabeth, 2
Virgil:
  Eclogues, 154, 175
  Aeneid, 166-67

Waller, Gary, 4, 10
Watkins, W. B. C., 149n12
Watson, D. G., 9
Whitney George:
  A Choice of Emblemes, 142n8
Wind, Edgar, 10, 57n9
Winter's Tale, 80n18
Woodbridge, Linda, 100
Wyatt, Sir Thomas, 159
Wyndham, George, 55n7, 143

zeugma, 18, 70
Zeuxis, 111